KRISHNA JANMABHOOMI

TRUTH, DISPUTES & LEGAL STATUS

AF674637

KRISHNA JANMABHOOMI

TRUTH, DISPUTES & LEGAL STATUS

MAHEK MAHESHWARI

PRABHAT
PAPERBACKS

No part of this publication can be reproduced, stored in a retrieval system or transmitted in any form or by any means, electronic, mechanical, photocopying, recording or otherwise, without prior permission of the author. Rights of this book are with the author.

Published by
PRABHAT PAPERBACKS
An imprint of Prabhat Prakashan Pvt. Ltd.
4/19 Asaf Ali Road,
New Delhi-110002 (INDIA)
e-mail: prabhatbooks@gmail.com

ISBN 978-93-5521-199-6
KRISHNA JANMABHOOMI
by **Mahek Maheshwari**

© Reserved

Edition
First, 2022

Price
₹ 300 (Rupees Three Hundred Only)

Printed at
Nakshatra Art, Delhi

वन्दे गुरोः श्री चरणारविन्दम्

This book is dedicated to My Spiritual Master
A.C. Bhaktivedanta Swami Srila Prabhupada.
He lives forever by his divine instructions
and the followers live with him.

Foreword

Mahek Maheshwari has written an interesting book on the restoration of the Krishna Janmabhoomi Temple that was demolished by the Mughal fanatic Aurangzeb.

Mahek was introduced to me when he became an Intern in my Law Office. Now he has bloomed into an Advocate practicing law in New Delhi. In this book he has ably narrated the historical context of the demolition of the existing Krishna Janmabhoomi Temple and the subsequent, although incomplete, efforts of Hindus to recover the Janmabhoomi site and re-build the Temple.

However, unlike the Ramlala temple case [concluded in 2019 by the Supreme Court], for Krishna Janmabhoomi temple there are obstacles arising from Places of Worship (Special Provisions) Act, 1991 (hereinafter referred to as "PoW Act"). Presently my Writ Petition challenging the constitutionality of the 1991 Act is pending in the Supreme Court, after it was admitted and Notice issued.

In particular, Section 3 of the PoW Act bars conversion of places of worship with a cut off date of August 15, 1947.

Section 4 of the same Act declares that "If, on the commencement of this Act, any suit, appeal or other proceeding with respect to the conversion of the religious character of any place of worship, existing on the 15th day of August, 1947, is pending before any Court, tribunal or other authority, the same shall abate, and no suit, appeal or other proceeding with respect to any such matter shall lie on or after such commencement in any Court, tribunal or other authority..."

The two provisions of the PoW Act are open to two main objections grounded in constitutional law.

First, is the text of Article 13(2) of the Constitution:

"The State shall not make any law which takes away or abridges the rights conferred by this Part [Part – III] and any law made in contravention of this clause shall, to the extent of the contravention, be void."

This means that any legislation that Parliament passes must comply with the Constitution laid down fundamental rights. The significance of rights placed under Part III lies in the fact that the citizens can approach the court if a law is passed violating the right, to make its effect null and void.

This inference is derived from a combined reading of Articles 32 and 13(2) of the Constitution. The PoW

Act and in particular Section 4, however, takes away citizens' right to approach the court under Article 32 of the Constitution.

The right at issue can be found in at least three articles of the chapter on fundamental rights as well as in the Preamble.

"The State shall not deny to any person equality before the law or the equal protection of the laws within the territory of India." (Article 14)

"... all persons are equally entitled to freedom of conscience and the right freely to profess, practice and propagate religion." (Article 25)

Every religious denomination, or section, had the right to mange its own affairs in matters of religion. (Article 26)

"LIBERTY of thought, expression, belief, faith and worship." (Preamble)

For the purpose of our first contention, we're not concerned with Article 14. It will, however, form the part of our second contention.

The basis of our first argument lies in Articles 25, 26, and the preamble read with Articles 32 and 13(2) of the Constitution.

The position of Indian constitution based on a catena of Supreme Court judgments is that fundamental rights cannot be altered by any law passed by Parliament.

Justice Hidayatullah, in Sajjan Singh, remarked that the nature of rights guaranteed under Part III cannot simply be envisaged as mere "playthings of a special majority."

This is to say that an Act passed by the Parliament – the Places of Worship Act, in this case – cannot annihilate my fundamental right of freedom of worship enshrined under Articles 25 and 26, as well as text of the Preamble, and the judicial review thereof.

Secondly, the singular exception to the provisions of Section 4 of the Act, as stated in section 5 of the Act, was the Ram Janmabhoomi case. Before proceeding with the analysis let us reproduce the exact wording of Section 5 of the Act:

Nothing contained in this Act shall apply to the place or place of worship commonly known as Ram Janma-Bhoomi-Babri Masjid situated in Ayodhya in the State of Uttar Pradesh and to any suit, appeal or other proceeding relating to the said place or place of worship.

A convincing argument can be made that the PoW Act is discriminatory for two reasons: (i) it leaves out other – but of similar essential importance such as the birthplace of Lord Krishna in Mathura or Lord Shiva's Jyotirlinga in the Gyanwapi premises – religious sites from being reclaimed by the community which, it believes, are occupied by another; and (ii) the cut-off date of 15 August 1947 is arbitrary.

The Supreme Court in Royappa held that "equality is antithetic to arbitrariness. In fact equality and arbitrariness are sworn enemies; one belongs to the rule of law in a republic while the other, to the whim and caprice of an absolute monarch. Where an act is arbitrary it is implicit in it that it is unequal both according to political logic and constitutional law, and is therefore violative of Article 14."

What is at issue here is the content of Article 14, which guarantees equality before law and equal protection of laws to all individuals. Under the two-pronged Article 14 test, first settled by the Indian Supreme Court in Anwar Ali Sarkar, any legislative classification that allocates advantages and disadvantages on a differential ground, will be unconstitutional unless:

(a) there is intelligible differentia between the classification made, which distinguishes those that are grouped together from those that have been excluded;

(b) that differentia must have a rational relation to the object sought to be achieved by the statute in question.

Keeping this in mind, I argue that Section 5 of the PoW Act fails to satisfy the conventional classification test of Article 14.

A combined reading of Section 4 and 5 makes it apparently clear that the Act makes an arbitrary eligibility criteria for religious sites to be reclaimed by the group which, it believes, are occupied by another. It allows, by the way of Section 5, only the hitherto Shri Ram Janmabhoomi Temple dispute to be reclaimed.

The classification made under the PoW Act leaves out several other religious sites having similar essential importance (such as the birthplace of Lord Krishna in Mathura or Lord Shiva's Jyotirlinga in in the Gyanwapi premises.)

Taking into account these exclusions, one may refer to "maintenance of secular fabric of the nation" and that such classification is made to avoid litigation and communal conflicts. However, such a classification is not based on an intelligible differentia for two primary reasons, and therefore unconstitutional.

First, the exception made in favour of Shri Ram Janmabhoomi presumes the rights of the parties attached to the Ayodhya dispute more equal and holier than the rights of similarly placed parties in relation to other religious sites.

Second, the classification is devoid of any factual basis and based on a premise that the termination of legal proceedings for reclamation of religious sites other than Shri Ram Janmabhoomi will ease communal tension in the country. Needles to say, a routine law and order situation cannot be the basis for suspension of a constitutional right.

For these reasons, the classification is offensive and not based on an intelligible differentia. Considering that the classification fails to conform with the intelligible differentia test; it may next be argued that the object of the Act bears a rational nexus with the differentiation it has created – the second prong of the test. This counter argument, however, will not pass the scrutiny for two reasons (i) in Subramanain Swamy vs CBI, the Supreme Court has added another prong to the rational nexus requirement, by observing that the object that the statute seeks to achieve should itself be legitimate.

That is to say, a discriminatory classification cannot be justified on the ground that it has a rational nexus with the aim that the statute seeks to achieve; (ii) as per the four-pronged test of proportionality, the State is required to demonstrate that its restriction placed on the fundamental right is narrowly tailored to achieve the goal, or at the very least, is important enough and proportionate to the intended goal.

Additionally, the cut-off date of 15 August 1947 is a reflection of colonial continuity. The Constitution – in the words of Granville Austin – was "a social document." That is, it is a transformative document.

The cut-off date made under the PoW Act, on the other hand, views Independence and Constitution as a colonial continuity – an antithesis to the constitutional norms of equality and fairness, henceforth arbitrary.

For the reasons discussed above, the Places of Worship Act can be declared as unconstitutional and hence not an obstacle to restoring the Lord Krishna Janmabhoomi in Mathura which is presently under a mosque.

Hence, Mahek Maheshwari's book has come out at the right time and is a must read book.

– **Dr. Subramanian Swamy**
Former Member of Parliament
Economist & Harvard Professor

❑

Author's Note

This book is the outcome with the sole intention to provide the clearer view with regard to the position of Krishna Janmasthan and Shahi Idgah Mosque. I was inspired by journalist Mr. Sandeep Deo to write this book so that Readers may arrive at a conclusion themselves with regard to status quo of the disputed site whether it is Temple or that of Mosque.

Mathura being my maternal home and a place where I feel most blissful had excited me since childhood to explore more and more about it. It's a center of art, culture, religion, food, archaeological and historical remains etc.

I got proposal by journalist Sandeep Deo ji as a question that if I had inclination into law and spirituality with deep connection with Mathura, where I had been also appeared in Ayodhya Ram Mandir Case along with Dr. Subramanian Swamy then why I am not writing any book on Krishna Janmabhoomi? On this I gave a thought and started the work after contemplation all alone and with my close friends and mentors along with the blessings of my elders.

This book encompasses vividly the historical facts with regard to Krishna Janmabhoomi & Shahi Idgah Mosque, legal position what is and what should be.

It's not only about the historical facts but then also about the Islamic law, Hindu Dharmshastras, culture & practices and above all a broader picture in the light of the Constitution of India.

Efforts had been made to keep this book as a complete package of historical, philosophical and legal treatise with a flow and language that even the layman could assimilate it.

The successful completion of this book wouldn't have been possible if my friends, CA finalist Shreshtha Chaudhary and Pratishtha Chaudhary have not spared their valuable time for formatting this book.

❑

Contents

Holi Gate, Mathura

CHAPTER 1

Mathura and its Glories

> *To Other Countries, I may go as a Tourist.*
> *But to India, I come as a Pilgrim.*
>
> **—Martin Luther King**

Mathura is a district of Uttar Pradesh State of North-Central India. Mathura city is situated along the banks of Yamuna River, and a part of Agra Division. The District is bounded on the northeast by Aligarh District, on the southeast by Hathras District, on the south by the Agra District, the west by Rajasthan and northwest by Haryana State. Mathura is an important pilgrimage centre of Hindu Dharma.

The city is located approximately 160 kilometres south-east of Delhi, and 60 kilometres north of Agra, about 20 kilometres from Goverdhan and 14 kilometres from Vrindavan.

Mathura has an ancient history and is the homeland and birthplace of Lord Shri Krishna who was born in the Yadu Dynasty.

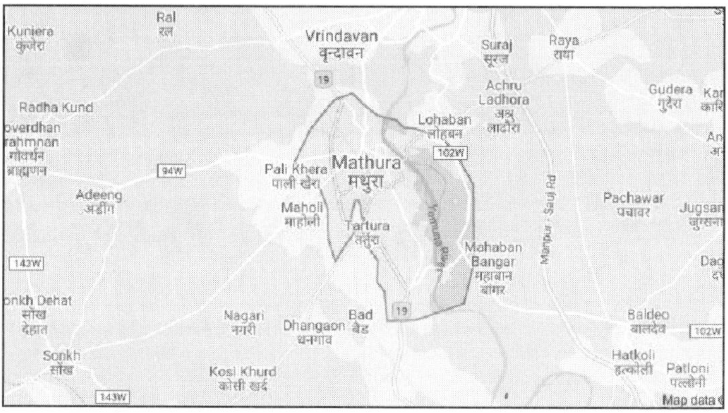

According to history, the city is also known with different names like, **Madhupuri; The capital of Braja, Madhuvan.**

As it is mentioned in the oldest Indian epic; **The Ramayan.** One of the Raghuvanshi prince Shatr-ughan slays a demon called Lavanasura. Afterwards, the place came to be known as Madhuvan as it was thickly wooded. Many scriptures describe it as **Madhupuri** which is among Saptpuris famous for Liberation (Moksha), gradually it became known as **Mathura**.

(Shatrughan slays Lavansur)

Madhyatetujagatsarva brahma gyanena yen va
Tatsaarbhutamyatasyaa Mathura sanigadhyate
(Gopal Tapani Upanishad - Uttara Khand 72)

The foundation of this absolute Knowledge, Brahmajnana, which pervades this entire creation is Sri Mathurapuri, implying that Sri Mathura is the source of all Absolute Knowledge and Devotion.

However, here, in the auspicious land of Braja, knowledge becomes submerged into an incredible ocean of bliss.

According to Padma Purana, Sri Mathura, the birthplace of our beloved Lord Sri Krishna, is placed as one the seven major ancient cities famous for granting salvation. This city is a sacred and blessed city.

Ayodhya Mathura maya kashi kanchi Avantika
Puridwaravatichaivasaptaitaa moksha dayika

Where is the doubt of its supremacy over Vaikuṇṭha? The fifth goal of life is Kṛṣṇa-prema or love of God. The first four goals of life are dharma, artha, kāma, and moksa, (religiosity, wealth, sense gratification and liberation). The first goal begins to sprout by staying here only one day, then what to speak of other material benefits?

Aho madhupuri dhanya vaikunthaygariyasi
Deenmaikamnivaasenaharau bhakti prajayate

There are seven great cities in the Indian subcontinent.

Amongst these, only Sri Mathura received the honour of becoming the birthplace of Krishna; this is most famous land where the personification of eternity, knowledge and bliss (Sat-cid-ānanda) appeared, complete with all sixteen attributes, ever protected by the divine and invincible armour of Sahasradhāri. Then, where is the doubt of this land's characteristics being celebrated as supernatural, beyond the realm of maya? This land exists throughout the four yugas. There are ample proofs available in vedic scriptures to substantiate this fact.

Towards the end of Satya-yuga, a demon called Madhu became master of the three worlds after defeating all Demi-gods.

The Demi-gods were terrified by the atrocities of this demon and approached the Lord for protection. The Lord, after fighting a fierce battle, which lasted for 10 years, killed Madhu.

The Demi-gods praised the Lord and addressed Him with a new name, Madhava, renaming Madhupurī as Mathura. Eighty four holy places were established here by the gods.

Valmiki Ramayana, Mahabharata and Harivamsa Purana label Mathura as Madhura or Madhupuri. According to Vishnu Purana, in Treta-yuga, Shatrughan killed Lavanasura, son of Madhu and established Mathura city after clearing a dense forest.

According to Vishnu Purana:

Hatva cha lavanamrakshomadhuputrammahabalam
Shatrughnomadhra naam puri yatra chakaarvai

Sukadeva in Bhagvatam:

Satrughnas ca madhoputralavaanamarakasam
hatvamadhuvanecakremathuranamavaipurim

Shatrughan also killed a Raksasa named Lavana, who was the son of Madhu Raksasa. Thus, he established the town known as Mathura in the great forest known as Madhuvana.

(Srimad Bhagvatam 9.11.14)

Hitvavana tat Saumitraha

(Harivamsa Purana 1.54-55)

This implies that Shatrughan clears the forest of Madhuvana and established a new residential estate named Mathura and ruled it for twelve years. Some scholars believe that the newly founded city by Shatrughan was named Surasena city.

At the fagged end of Dvapara, Mathura gained unprecedented significance by becoming the birthplace of our dear Lord Krishna and later Kamsa's end happened here. In the Kali-yuga, it survived devastations again and again and our history and people are the proof.

Therefore, the existence of this holy city in all four yugas is an established fact.

(Adi VarahaPurana 168-9, 158-1, Harivamsha Purana 1.54.55)

Varaha Bhagavan said to the Earth: My Mathura Mandala covering over 80 kosas or 210 km. is a widely spread estate. Here, one gets the fruit of an Asvamedha Yajna at every step, and by taking bath, is relieved of all sins.

In the Puranas, it is called Mathura Mandala. Hiuen Tsang came to Mathura in year 635 A.D. and recorded the area of Mathura as 833 miles or 1230 kilometers. Mathura, Bharatapur, Karoli, Dhaulpur, Agra and half of the northern part of Gwalior state used to be included in Mathura state. The area of Mathura city has been recorded as 5 kilometers.

After the Lord's pastimes, this place almost became extinct. In Kali-yuga, Sri Caitanya Mahaprabhu came here along with Rupa Goswami and others, rediscovering the lost places of the pastimes of Krishna enacted in this locality.

Narada reveals in great detail the importance of Mathura in Garga-samhita, Mathurakanda, Mathura Mahatamya, before King Bahulasva, in 39 verses. Who is the presiding deity of Mathura? Who is the minister? Who is the guard? Who is the enjoyer?

Narada says:

svayahi mathuranathah kesava klesha nashanah

Kesava, Himself being the famous Lord of Mathura, extinguishes all troubles, and is also named Varahadeva.

The Lord presented this Deity of Kesavadeva initially to the Brahmin Kapiladeva, from Kapiladeva to Indra, then to Ravana. Later, Sri Rama brought Him to Ayodhya; Satrughna received Him from Sri Rama and later enshrined Him in Mathura. The same Kesava-Varaha became the Supreme Ruler of Mathura.

kshatashreemathurayashchanamnabhutesh
varahshivah
vadandampatkinebhaktyarthammantratamvrajet

The compassionate Guardian of Mathurā is BhūteśvaraMahādeva, who is looked upon as the security force of Mathurā.

(Garga Samhita Mathura Mahatmya 25.9)

Mathurayam cha deva tvamkshetrapalobhavishyasi
Tvayidrashtemahadeva mama kshetraphalambhavet

Krishna says: Deva, You will be the guardian of Mathura. Hey Mahadeva! Your audience will grant men My Eternal Abode.

Sri Bhutesvara, the benevolent guardian of Mathura punishes the sinners and initiates them into bhakti.

(Vayu Purana 168.5, 168.6)

Brahma gets his illustrious son, Svayambhuva after performing austerities in this land; Varuna attains salvation, Lord Rama wins victory over Lavanasura; Ravana gains victory over all the gods; and Santanu got Bhisma as his son.

All of them were successful on account of the auspiciousness of this land. Simply by saying of the name Mathurā, one gains the same benefit as chanting Krsna's name; even casually hearing its name grants the fruit of hearing the transcendental topics of Krsna's pastimes.

In spite of being unknowingly touched by its Holy dust of Mathura, it is still equivalent to a saint's auspicious touch and being submitted to its various smells is likened to the purifying potency of smelling a Tulasi leaf; and just imagine.....if one fortunately visits Mathura... what a blessing! This would be like having Krsna's personal association! Mukti (liberation) is roaming in every street of this city, waiting for fortunate candidates!

(Garga Samhita Mathura Khanda 25.25, 26, 32, 33)

Among the seven great cities, Mathura is most auspicious, because only it grants liberation in four various ways:

Either by simply taking birth here, performing the ceremony for wearing a sacred thread, meeting one's death here or if the last rites of a departing soul are performed in Mathura. Any one of these four activities grants liberation to a living entity, the ultimate reason being that this land is sanctified due to the appearance of Krishna, which increases a million times the good fortune of Mathura once again, (Krsna comes to Mathura every 8,406,000,000 years!).

Mathura is the holiest city because Krishna spent eleven most blissful years with the Brajavasis in Gokula, mesmerizing them with His enchanting pastimes and saturating their heart with His affection. Krishna arrives here with Akruraji. After hearing about the entrance of these two extraordinary brothers, elegantly adorned in yellow and blue garments, whose presence enhances the glory of Mathura, the women folk of the city, quickly and eagerly ran to witness their beautiful forms.

They have been keenly waiting for this rare chance of seeing Krishna and Balarama for such a long time that they enthusiastically gathered in the balconies of high buildings, not even bothering to dress up properly.

Every street of this opulent city is filled with the most fragrant flowers and who knows which thoroughfare would be the luckiest one to receive this blessed vision. Seeing Krishna, the Lord of the whole world, surrounded by the Gopas, these fortunate women lose all external consciousness, their gaze being fixed only on His charming lotus face.

This district of Mathura is not just what we are able to see with our physical eyes, but is totally and eternally filled and pulsating with the divine playful pastimes of Krishna, the ultimate friend of the fallen souls. In order to avoid any of the offenses in this holy place, we should always cautiously remember that all of its Holy places including bathing places, hills, magnificent buildings, people, birds, animals, plants, trees, in other words, all living entities, Yamuna and Giriraja etc., are factually, eternally and transcendentally divine and not otherwise.

The amazing form of Mathura appears just like a lotus. The presiding Deity Kesavadeva is sitting in the whorl of this lotus, on the western petal; Harideva is having His pastime on Goverdhana hill; the northern petal holds the attractive form of Govinda deva in Vrindavana; on the southern petal, the awesome form of Varahadeva is residing in Mathura; and on the eastern petal, Lord Visranti is being worshipped. Braja is still the source of India's spiritual power, actually not only of India, but, of the whole universe.

Brajasamudra mathura kamalrmakarand;
brajabanita sab kumudhai kairavgokulachand

Braja is an ocean of love.... Mathura is the lotus growing there.... Vrindavana is the whorl of this lotus.... The Gopis are the nectar of this lotus.... and Krsna is the bee relishing this precious nectar!

(AdiVaraha Purana 163.15, 16)

Mathura is also important from the view point of glorious Sikh Community as Guru Nanak Dev Ji visited Mathura-Vrindavan during the Shravan Fair, where he noticed people were struggling for clean drinking water in that humid atmosphere since the water of the river Yamuna had become muddy due to the previous day's rainstrom. Seeing the condition of the crowd, Guru Nanak Dev Ji himself established a water stall quenching thirst of thousand of visitors.

After this incident a shrine was established by Udasi Priests on the bank of river Yamuna which is currently known as **"Gurudwara Guru Nanak Sahib Bagichi''.**

ECONOMY AND INDUSTRY

A. Oil Refinery

Mathura city is the major contributor in the economy of Uttar Pradesh. The 6th refinery of Indian Oil was commissioned in 1982 with a capacity of 6.0 MMTPA to meet the demand of petroleum products in the north western region of the country. Mathura Refinery is having its own captive power plant, which was augmented with the commissioning of three Gas Turbines (GT) and Heat Recovery Steam Generator (HRSG) in phases from 1997 to 2005 using Natural Gas (NG) as fuel to take care of environment.

B. Production of Milk Products

The city is also a hub for production of milk based sweets prominent among them being Mathura

Pedas. Mathura has many milk trading centres where you can buy any amount of fresh milk.

C. **Textile Printing And Cotton Production**

Dyeing and printing of cottons are one of the biggest business in Mathura that also includes sari-printing. The city has been renowned as one of the largest centre for the production of bleached cotton materials. Also, silver ornaments manufacturing are major industrial contributors to the region. Majority of these silver ornaments include silver jewelry and statues for gods and goddesses.

The city is also involved in other big businesses that employs a large part of population in these industries.

TOURISM

Mathura is a holy place for Hindus. There are many religious as well as historic places in the city; the major one is **Vrindavan**. As all know that Mathura is homeplace of Lord Shri Krishna and he is very famous for all his avatars and forms. Some holy places in city are-

- Shri Krishna Janmabhoomi
- Vishram Ghat; Bank of River Yamuna
- Shri Bhuteshwar Mahadev Temple
- Birla Temple

- Keshav Dev Temple
- Iskcon Temple, Vrindavan
- Prem Mandir, Vrindavan
- Vrindavan Chandrodaya Mandir, Vrindavan
- Banke Bihari Temple, Vrindavan
- Rangeshwar Temple
- Dwarkadhish Temple

The local language of Mathura is Braj-Bhasha and also spoken in the other parts of several states in India.

- **Shri Krishna Janmabhoomi**

  This is a Hindu temple and birthplace of Lord Shri Krishna.

  Beside the Krishna Janmabhoomi, the Keshava Dev temple is situated where spiritual environment could be felt.

This temple shares its boundary with the Shahi Eidgah Mosque which is built after demolishing the Keshava Dev Temple and the Jail compartment where Lord Krishna is originally believed to have appeared.

- **Dwarkadhish Temple**

This is also a Hindu temple which is built up by Seth Gokul Das Parikh; the treasurer of Gwalior in 1814. Lord Krishna also worshipped here in the form of Dwarkadhish. The temple has large premises in the main market of Mathura City. It has richly carved pillars and beautiful paintings on the ceilings.

- **Shri Bhuteshwar Mahadev Temple**

This temple is dedicated to Lord Shiva. It is very ancient and one of the prominent temple in Mathura city. According to the brajwasis, the temple shields the city from evil and also known as Protector Lord of Mathura.

- **Iskcon Temple**

Sri Krishna Balrama Temple was built by ISKCON Founder Acharya V.C. Bhaktivedanta Swami Srila Prabhupada in 1975. The temple is located in Vrindavan about 14 km from Mathura City.

The temple stands near the banks of River Yamuna and has magnificent structure which attracts everyone. It is beautiful inside and also has peaceful environment. Many locals call it – ''HARE KRISHNA HARE RAMA TEMPLE.''

- **Vishram Ghat**

  This is a worship place of Hindus situated on the banks of River Yamuna where pilgrims take bath in the holy river. This is one of the prominent ghat in all other ghats in whole Braj region.

- **Banke Bihari Temple**

  Shri Banke Bihari is also another form of Lord Krishna which is situated in Vrindavan near Mathura. This is one of the oldest and prominent temples among other 7 Goswami's Temples.

  Shri Banke Bihari originally manifested by Swami Haridas in Nidhivan; Vrindavan itself.

The term Banke means 'Bent' and Bihari means 'Enjoyer'.

- **Radharaman Temple**

Another form of Lord Shri Krishna, this is one of the divine and ancient temple in Vrindavan.

Radharaman means 'the one who gives pleasure to Radha'.

The temple was established in 1542 and the Shri Vigrah (Deity) was self manifested from Shaligram (one of the Lord Vishnu forms).

This temple is one of the 6 principal Goswami's temple - Shri Gopal Bhatt Goswami.

❑

Bhagwan
Shri Krishna

CHAPTER 2

Shri Krishna Mythical or Historical

"Vasudeva then saw the newborn child, who had very wonderful lotus like eyes and who bore in His four hands the four weapons Sankha, Cakra, Gadā and Padma. On His chest was the mark of Srīvatsa and on His neck the brilliant Kaustubha gem. Dressed in yellow, His body blackish like a dense cloud, His scattered hair fully grown, and His helmet and earrings sparkling uncommonly with the valuable gem Vaidurya, the child, decorated with a brilliant belt, armlets, bangles and other ornaments, appeared very wonderful."

(Srimad-Bhagvatam 10.3.9-10)

Shri Krishna; The supreme personality of godhead is the most worshippable deity in Hinduism. He was appeared in Mathura; the day popuraly known as Krishna Janamashtmi. The name KRISHNA means ***"All Attractive"***.

"krsnas tu bhagavan svayam" - Lord Krishna is the original personality of Godhead.

(Srimad-Bhagvatam 1.3.28)

"sac-cid-ananda-vigrahaḥ" – Lord Krishna has an eternal blissful spiritual body.

(Sri Brahma-samhita 5.1)

Shri Krishna was appeared 5,000 years ago and performs his transcendental pastimes for 125 years before returing to his abode. He is known by different names and devotees worship him in different forms like-

- Dwarikadhish
- Vitthal
- Banke Bihari
- Shrinathji
- Jagannath
- Radharaman

As per the different pastimes of Lord Krishna he has innumerable names as, he himself is unlimited being supreme personality of godhead. There is no limit to the glories of the holy names of Lord Krishna. It is said by one of the prominent Acharya named Srila Bhaktivinod Thakura of Gaudiya Vaishnav School/Sampradaya of Vaishnaism.

"Anant Krsner Nama anant Mahima Narad adi Vyasdeva dite naare seema"

There are infinite holy names of Lord Krishna with infinite Glories that Even great saints/devotees Like Narada and and Vyasdeva(Compiler of Vedas) can't bound their limits.

"Fools deride Me when I descend in the human form. They do not know My transcendental nature as the Supreme Lord of all that be."

(Lord Krishna, Bhagavad-Gita 9.11).

When Lord Krishna appears on planet earth in His original human like form, which is eternal and spiritual, not material. The foolish think of Him as an ordinary person and neglect Him.

They compare themselves with God, and because they have limitations due to their material body, they conclude that God cannot have a form, because He is great. They fail to realize that God has an eternal spiritual form, and not a temporary material form like ours. It's for this reason that He is great, and we are not.

As previously described that Lord Shri Krishna has innumerable forms. According to Sanatan Dharma, the cycle of time is known as **Divya Yug or Chatur Yug,** which has been further classified into Satyug, Tretayug, Dwaparyug, Kaliyug.

A. SATYUG

The process of God Realization was **Tapasya or Dhyan** or **Meditation** of Lord Vishnu (Krte Dhyayte Vishnu).

In this age, Lord Krishna (Vishnu) has appeared in the forms of Varah Avatar (Boar Incarnation), Kurma Avatar (Tortoise like Incarnation), Narsimha Avatar (Half Man-Half Lion Incarnation) and Matsya Avatar (Fish like Incarnation).

The life span of human in this era is about 1,00,000 years.

Varah-Dev

Kurma-Dev

Narsimha-Dev

Matsya-Dev

'Krita Yug' describes in Mahabharat Epic such as-

There were no poor and no rich; there was no need to labor, because all that men required was obtained by the power of will; the chief virtue was the abandonment of all worldly desires. The Krita

Yuga was without disease; there was no lessening with the years; there was no hatred or vanity, or evil thought; no sorrow, no fear. All mankind could attain to supreme blessedness.

(Vana Parva)

B. TRETAYUG

The process of God Realization was **Performing of Sacrifices** (Yajna) for the pleasure of Lord Vishnu (Tretayam Yajto Makhaye).

In this age, Lord Krishna (Vishnu) has appeared in the forms of Lord Vaman (Dwarf Like Incarnation), Lord Parshuram, Lord Rama whose birthplace is Ayodhya; presently is in Uttar Pradesh of which long fought legal battle in the Supreme Court of India, the verdict of which has been granted in the favour of Sanatan Dharmas. On the disputed site of Ayodhya, now a grand Ram temple is in the process of construction.

The life span of human in this era is about 10,000 years.

C. DVAPARAYUG

The process of God Realization was Deity Worship for the pleasure of Lord Vishnu **(Dvapare Paricharyayam)**.

The life span of human in this era is about 1,000 years.

Vaman-Dev

Sri Parshuram

Sri Ramchandra

In this age, Lord Krishna is the supreme personality of godhead from whom all other incarnations or plenary portions of such incarnations appears.

(Srimad Bhagvatam 1.3.28)

Shri Krishna spoke in Srimad Bhagvat Gita -

yadā yadā hi dharmasya
glānir bhavati bhārata
abhyutthānam adharmasya
tadātmānaṁ sṛjāmy aham

Whenever and wherever, there is a decline in religious practice, O descendant of Bharata, and a predominant rise of irreligion – at that time I descend Myself.

(Bhagavad-Gita 4.7)

paritrāṇāya sādhūnāṁ
vināśāya ca duṣkṛtām
dharma-saṁsthāpanārthāya
sambhavāmi yuge yuge

To deliver the pious and to annihilate the miscreants, as well as to reestablish the principles of religion,

I Myself appear, millennium after millennium.

(Bhagavad-Gita 4.8)

Shri Krishna's Appearance (Birth of Shri Krishna)

Lord Krishna first appeared in the form of Four handed Vishnu in front of Sri Vasudev and Devaki in the prison house of Kansa in Mathura.

Currently this prison house is demolished and Shahi Eidgah Majid built over the same. After giving darshan in the form of Narayan, Afterwards, Shri Krishna took a divine form of child and consequently he entered in the womb of Mother Devaki.

This shows he is transcendental nature of his appearance/birth, which undoubtedly proves he is the supreme personality of godhead.

After his appearance, Sri Vasudev transfered him to Gokul in the house of Nand and Yashoda in exchange for Yashoda's girl child.

Nandas tv atmaja utpanne jatahlado maha-manah

"When Lord Sri Krsna appeared as his son, Nanda Maharaja was overwhelmed with jubilation."

Ahuya vipran veda-jan snatah sucir alankrtah/ vacayitva svastyayanam jata-karmatmajasya vai

"Then Nanda Maharaja arranged to have the Vedic birth ceremony [jata-karma] celebrated for his newborn child."

(Srimad Bhagvatam 10.5.1–2)

Goverdhan Lila (Lifting of Goverdhan Hill)

There was a tradition in Braj of worshipping the King of heaven - Indra; who is responsible for supplying rain. One day Shri Krishna asked his father Sri Nandbaba about this vedic tradition of worshipping Indra and after many conversations between them, Shri Nand replied this is our duty to perform such vedic sacrifices as we are farmers we need water and Indra is a ruling deity of water.

Upon hearing this, Shri Krishna replied that real supplier of everything to us and to our cows is Goverdhan Hill. He supplies us everything that we need in our life like - Fresh green grass for our cows, Sweet drinking water, tasty fruits and vegetables, so why we should not worship Goverdhan instead of Indra because it is the duty of Indra to supply water to everyone including oceans. Also, Goverdhan is one of the form of Sri Vishnu.

In this way, Shri Krishna convinced everyone to worship Goverdhan. Krishna's words being very sweet and was spoken in a way of Karma-mimarsa philosophy as per our scriptures.

During the worship of Goverdhan, Demigod Indra showed his wrath by sending his Samvartak clouds and devouring the whole Braj with extensive flood. Shri Krishna protected the Brajwasis by lifting the Goverdhan Hill of 7 kos i.e., 21 kms on the little finger of His left hand and he did it continuously for 7 days and 7 nights. This shows again that Krishna is transcendental in nature and so His abode Brajmandal.

Krishna shows his inconceivable power

Lord Krishna performed many miracles which have never been perfomed by anyone in his childhood that shows that he is supreme personality of godhead. During his childhood pastimes, he saved his friends and other brajwasis from many demons like Aghasura, Putna, Shaktasura, Bakasura, Aristasura, Trunavrata, Dhenukasura sent by Maharaj Kansa and also save life of Brajwasis from the huge and several hooded snake Kaliya.

Bakasura Vadh

Kaliya Mardhan

Aristasura Vadh

Dhenukasura Vadh

Trunavrata Vadh

Putna Vadh

Kurukshetra War

About 5,000 years ago, the Mahabharat War took place on the land of Kurukshetra between Pandvas and Kauravas. In the battlefield, when Arjuna seeing his relatives on the opposite side his heart was not willing to kill their love ones and he put down his Gandiv (Arjun's bow).

After seeing his delusion, Shri Krishna guided him on the path of his duties and responsibilities towards Dharma. Then, Shri Krishna spoke the Bhagavad Gita; Song of Supreme Personality of Godhead.

The main reason of delusion of Arjuna was his bodily relationship with the opposite armies in Kurukshetra.

Upon seeing this, Shri Krishna explained to Arjuna that he is not the body which is temporary and destructible. But, beyond his body that is Soul which is permanent so he should not lament over his bodily relationships and perform his duty as a warrior in which if he wins he will enjoy the kingdom and if he loses he will be transferred to a higher planet, so there should be no cause of lamentation.

tasmāt sarveṣu kāleṣu
mām anusmara yudhya ca
mayy arpita-mano-buddhir
mām evaiṣyasy asaṁśayaḥ

Therefore, Arjuna, you should always think of Me in the form of Krishna and at the same time carry out your prescribed duty of fighting. With your activities dedicated to Me and your mind and intelligence fixed on Me, you will attain Me without doubt.

This instruction to Arjuna is very important for all men engaged in material activities. The Lord does not say that one should give up his prescribed duties or engagements. One can continue them and at the same time think of Lord by chanting Holy names. This will free one from material contamination and engage the mind and intelligence in God. By chanting Lord's names, one will be transferred to the supreme planet, Krishnalok/ Goloka, without a doubt.

(Bhagavad-Gita 8.7)

Later on, Arjuna understood his duties and accorded with the instructions of the Lord Krishna for the performance of duty as a warrior by replying to Krishna with words-

arjuna uvāca
naṣṭo mohaḥ smṛtir labdhā
tvat-prasādān mayācyuta
sthito 'smi gata-sandehaḥ
kariṣye vacanaṁ tava

Arjuna said: My dear Kṛṣṇa, O infallible one, my illusion is now gone. I have regained my memory by Your mercy. I am now firm and free from doubt and am prepared to act according to Your instructions.

(Bhagavad-Gita 18.73)

In this way, Arjuna fought valiantly and Pandavas won the War.

D. KALIYUG

This present day and age is of Kaliyuga. The predominant character of this age is quarrel and hypocrisy. Srimad Bhagavatam mentions:

प्रायेणाल्पायुष: सभ्य कलावस्मिन् युगे जना: ।
मन्दा: सुमन्दमतयो मन्दभाग्या ह्युपद्रुता: ॥ १० ॥

O learned one, in this iron Age of Kali men almost always have but short lives. They are quarrelsome, lazy, misguided, unlucky and, above all, always disturbed.

(Srimad Bhagavatam 1.1.10)

कलौ तद्धरिकीर्तनात्

The process of deliverance in this age is Congregational chanting of Harinaam or holy name.

(Srimad Bhagavatam 12.3.52)

A similar verse is found in the Viṣṇu Purāṇa (6.2.17), and also in the Padma Purāṇa (Uttara-khaṇḍa 72.25) and the Bṛhan-nāradīya Purāṇa (38.97):

dhyāyan kṛte yajan yajñais
tretāyāṁ dvāpare 'rcayan
yad āpnoti tad āpnoti
kalau saṅkīrtya keśavam

"Whatever is achieved by meditation in Satya-yuga, by the performance of sacrifice in Tretā-yuga, and by the worship of Lord Kṛṣṇa's lotus feet in Dvāpara-yuga is obtained in the Age of Kali simply by glorifying the name of Lord Keśava."

Śrīla Jīva Gosvāmī has further quoted from the Brahma-vaivarta Purāṇa concerning the degraded condition of people in Kali-yuga:

ataḥ kalau tapo-yoga-
vidyā-yajñādikāḥ kriyāḥ
sāṅgā bhavanti na kṛtāḥ
kuśalair api dehibhiḥ

"Thus in the Age of Kali the practices of austerity, yoga meditation, Deity worship, sacrifice and so on, along with their various subsidiary functions, are not properly carried out, even by the most expert embodied souls."

Śrīla Jīva Gosvāmī has also cited the *Cāturmāsya-māhātmya* of the *Skanda Purāṇa* concerning the necessity of chanting Hare Kṛṣṇa in this age:

tathā caivottamaṁ loke
tapaḥ śrī-hari-kīrtanam
kalau yuge viśeṣeṇa
viṣṇu-prītyai samācaret

"In this way the most perfect penance to be executed in this world is the chanting of the name of Lord Śrī Hari. Especially in the Age of Kali, one can satisfy the Supreme Lord Viṣṇu by performing saṅkīrtana."

go-koöi-dänaà grahaëe khagasya
prayäga-gaìgodaka-kalpa-väsaù
yajïäyutaà meru-suvarëa-dänaà
govinda-kérter na samaà çatäàçaiù

"Even if one distributes ten million cows in charity during an eclipse of the sun, lives at the confluence of

the Ganges and Yamunä for millions of years, or gives a mountain of gold in sacrifice to the brahmanas, he does not earn one hundredth part of the merit derived from chanting Hare Krishna." In other words, one who accepts the chanting of Hare Krishna to be some kind of pious activity is completely misled. Of course, it is pious; but the real fact is that Krishna and His name, being transcendental, are far above all mundane pious activity. Pious activity is on the material platform, but chanting of the holy name of Krishna is completely on the spiritual plane. Therefore, although pasandis do not understand this, pious activity can never compare to the chanting of the holy name.

- **Kali-Santarana Upanishad:**

"Hare krishna hare krishna krishna krishna hare hare
hare rama hare rama rama rama hare hare
iti sodasakam namnam kali-kalmasa-nasanam
natah parataropayah sarva-vedesu drsyate"

'After searching through all the Vedic literature, one cannot find a method of religion more sublime for this age than the chanting of Hare Krishna.'

(quoted in Chaitanya Charitamrita, Adi-lila 3.40, Purport)

- **Brihan-naradiya Purana:**

'For spiritual progress in this Age of Kali, there is no alternative, there is no alternative, there is no alternative to the holy name, the holy name, the holy name of the Lord.'

(quoted in Chaitanya Charitamrita, Adi-lila 7.76, Purport)

- **Narada-pancharatra:**

  'The essence of all Vedic knowledge—comprehending the three kinds of Vedic activity [karma-kanda, jñana-kanda and upasana-kanda], the chandas, or Vedic hymns, and the processes for satisfying the demigods—is included in the eight syllables Hare Krishna, Hare Krishna. This is the reality of all Vedanta. The chanting of the holy name is the only means to cross the ocean of nescience.'

  (quoted in Chaitanya Charitamrita, Adi-lila, 7.76, Purport)

- **Narayana-samhita:**

  In Dvapara-yuga one could satisfy Krishna or Vishnu only by worshiping Him gorgeously according to the pañcaratriki system (temple Deity worship), but in the Age of Kali one can satisfy and worship the Supreme Personality of Godhead Hari simply by chanting the holy name."

  (quoted in Chaitanya Charitamrita, Adi-lila 7.76, Purport)

- **Srimad-Bhagavatam, 12.3.51:**

  'My dear King, although Kali-yuga is an ocean of faults, there is still one good quality about this age:

Simply by chanting the Hare Krishna maha-mantra, one can become free from material bondage and be promoted to the transcendental kingdom.'

—Sukadeva Goswami

hare krishna hare krishna krishna krishna hare hare hare
rama hare rama rama rama hare hare
iti sodasakam namnam kali-kalmasa-nasanam natah
parataropayah sarva-vedesu drsyate

The sixteen names of the Hare Krishna *maha-mantra*: hare krishna hare krishna krishna krishna hare hare, hare rama hare rama rama rama hare hare destroy all the inauspiciousness of the age of Kali.

This is the conclusion of all the Vedas.

(Kali-santarana Upanisad from Krishna Yajur Veda)

sanketyam parihasyam va
stobham helanam eva va
vaikuntha-nama-grahanam
asesagha-haram viduh

One who chants the holy name of the Lord is immediately freed from the reactions of unlimited sins, even if he chants indirectly [to indicate something else], jokingly, for musical entertainment, or even neglectfully. This is accepted by all the learned scholars of the scriptures.

(Srimad-Bhagavatam, 6.2.14)

nama sankirtana deva tarakam brahma drsyate hare
krishna hare krishna krishna krishna hare hare
hare rama hare rama rama rama hare hare

The nama sankirtana (public chanting) of Hare Krishna maha-mantra delivers a complete revelation of all of spiritual reality.

(Brahmanda Purana 6.59-60)

mukti-hetuka tāraka haya 'rāma-nāma'
'kṛṣṇa-nāma' pāraka hañā kare prema-dāna

The holy name of Lord Rāma certainly gives liberation, but the holy name of Kṛṣṇa transports one to the other side of the ocean of nescience and at last gives one ecstatic love of Kṛṣṇa.

(Chaitanya-charitamrita, Antya-lila 3.257)

harir eva samaradhyah sarva deve suresvarah
hari nama maha mantrair nasyatpapa pisacakam

All the grievous sins of one who worships Lord Sri Hari, the Lord of all lords, and chants the holy name, the maha-mantra, are removed.

(Padma Purana, Svarga Khanda 50.6)

hare krishna hare krishna krishna krishna hare hare hare
rama hare rama rama rama hare hare
sodasaitani namani dvatrimsad varnakani hi
kalau yuge maha-mantrah sammato jivatarane
varjayitva tu namaitad durjanaih parikalpitam
chandobaddham susiddhanta viruddham nabhyaset

padam tarakam brahma-namaitad brahmana
gurunadina kalisantaranadyasu
sruti-svadhigatam hareh praptam sri brahma-sisyena
sri naradena dhimata namaitad-uttamam srauta-
paramparyena brahmanah utsrjyaitan-maha-mantram
ye tvanyat kalpitam padam mahanameti
gayanti te sastra-guru langhanah
tattva-virodha-sanprktam tadrsam daurjanam matam
sravatha pariharyam syadatma-hitarthina sada
hare krishna hare krishna krishna krishna hare hare hare
rama hare rama rama rama hare hare

'Hare krishna hare krishna krishna krishna hare hare, hare rama hare rama rama rama hare hare: This sixteen-name, thirty-two syllable mantra is the *maha-mantra* in the age of Kali by which all living beings can be delivered.

One should never abandon chanting this *maha-mantra* and take to other so-called purificatory processes which are practiced by rascals, or engage in chanting other metrical compositions of the name of Krishna that are against the pure conclusions of the scriptures, or are filled with rasabhasa. About this divinely spiritual *maha-mantra*, which delivers one from material existence, the original guru, Lord Brahma, has said, kali-santararadi srutite, ***"The srutis have declared this mantra to be the best means of deliverance in the age of Kali"***. Having all heard this from Brahma, the sons and disciples of Brahma, beginning with Narada, all accepted the Hare Krishna *maha-mantra* and, having meditated on it, attained perfection.'

(Ananta-samhita)
Ananta-samhita is part of the Narada Pancaratra)

hare krishna krsneti krsneti mukhyan mahascarya-
namavali-siddha-mantran krpa-murti-caitanya-deva
upagitan kadabhyasya vrndavane syan krtarth

'When will my heart become satiated by perfecting the chanting of the Hare Krishna maha-mantra in Sri Vrndavana Dhama, which the most merciful Sri Caitanyadeva personally chanted and distributed to the fallen souls out of compassion? This wonderful maha-mantra is mixed with the mellows of love and is the chief and the perfection of all other mantras. They are full of spiritual energies and glories.'

(Sri Vrindavana Mahimamrta by Srila Prabodhananda Sarasvati 17.89)

hare krishna rama nama gana dana karinim
soka moha lobha tapa sarva vigna nasinim

pada padma lubdha bhakta vrnda bhakti dayinim
gaura murtim asu naumi nama sutra dharinim

'He makes the gift of the song of the names 'Hare, Krishna and Rama', and destroys all obstacles such as sorrow, delusion, greed and suffering. He gives the devotional service of Lord Krishna to the multitude of devotees who are eager for the shelter of His lotus feet.

I fall down swiftly to offer my prostrated obeisances to the Lord in His golden form, who holds a string of meditation beads.'

(Srila Sarvabhauma Bhattacarya, Susloka-Satakam 23)

sri-radhar bhave ebe gora avatar
hare krishna nam gaura korila pracar

(Vasudev Ghosh's bhajan "Jaya Jagannatha Sacira-nandana", text 4) Chaitanya-bhagavata Madhya-khanda 23.75-80: (trans. Kusakratha Das)

The Lord personally taught them, "Please happily hear from Me the maha-mantra of Lord Krishna's names. It is:

"Hare Krishna Hare Krishna Krishna Krishna Hare Hare Hare Rama Hare Rama Rama Rama Hare Hare"

The Lord said, "Regularly chant japa of this maha-mantra.

In this way you will attain all perfections. Chant at any time and in any circumstance. There are no other rules for chanting. Gather together, five or ten, in your own homes, clap hands and sing kirtana of these holy names.

You may also sing these words:

hari haraye namah krishna yadavaya namah gopala govinda rama sri madhusudana

'I offer my respectful obeisances unto the Supreme Personality of Godhead, Krishna. He is the descendant of the Yadu family. Let me offer my respectful obeisances unto Gopala, Govinda, Rama and Sri Madhusudana.'

(Also see Chaitanya-charitamrita 2.26.64)

Gathering at home with parents, wife, and children, please sing kirtana in this way.

japato hari namani sthane sata-gunadhikah
atmanam ca punaty-uccair-japan srotrn-punati ca

'Compared to that person who is attached to chanting japa, the person who performs loud chanting of the holy name of Sri Hari is one hundred times better. This is because the person who chants japa purifies himself, whereas the person who chants the holy name loudly in kirtana purifies himself, all those who are with him, and everyone else who hear the holy vibration.'

(Naradiya Purana, Prahlada-vakya)

pasu-paksi-krma-adi balite na pare
sunile se harinama ta'ra saba tare
japile se krishna-nama apani se tare
ucca-sankirtane para-upakare kare
ata eva ucca kari' kirtana karile
sata-guna phala haya sarva-sastre bole

'The animals, birds, and insects cannot chant the holy name, but by hearing the holy name chanted they can benefit. Chanting the japa of the holy name of Krishna purifies oneself, but the loud sankirtana of the holy name of Krishna benefits all living beings. Therefore, loudly

chant the holy name of Krishna in kirtana, and you will get one hundred times the benefit of chanting japa. This is the verdict of all the sastras.'

(Chaitanya-bhagavata 1.16, Haridasa Thakura speaking)

'Listen my dear Misra, in Kali-yuga there is no need for severe penances or performance of opulent sacrifices; whoever worships the Supreme Lord Krishna, he will be crowned with fortune and success. So go back to your home and worship Lord Krishna with undeviating faith and attention, giving up falsehood and pretensions. By chanting the holy name of Lord Hari, Krishna, you will simultaneously obtain both the proper spiritual practice and the ultimate goal. In this age of quarrel and hypocrisy the only means of deliverance is chanting the holy name of the Lord. There is no other way. There is no other way. There is no other way. I am repeating this great chant for deliverance to you. This consists of sixteen names of the Supreme Lord with thirty two syllables:

"Hare Krishna Hare Krishna Krishna Krishna Hare Hare Hare Rama Hare Rama Rama Rama Hare Hare"

By constantly chanting and worshiping this Maha Mantra, your heart will feel the first blossoming of love and God; then gradually you will understand the truth about the proper spiritual path and the ultimate spiritual goal.'

(Chaitanya-bhagavata 1.14, Lord Caitanya Mahaprabhu speaking to Tapana Misra)

In his purport to Caitanya-bhagavata Bhaktisiddhanta Sarasvati says very clearly that Haridasa Thakura chanted either loudly or softly and that is why his cave became Vaikuntha.

Chaitanya-bhagavata 1.16.172:

tabe haridasa ganga-tire gopha kari'
thakena virale ahar-nisa krishna smari'

'Then Haridasa went and found a cave on the bank of the Ganges. He remembered Krishna day and night as he resided alone in the cave.'

Purport: "While remaining in a solitary cave on the bank of the Ganges at Phuliya, Srila Thakura Mahasaya loudly chanted the names of Krishna and passed his days and night remembering the pastimes of the Lord. Sometimes he would chant the sixteen name, thirty-two syllable, maha-mantra loudly (uccaihsvare), and sometimes he would chant softly (mrdusvare). Every day he would complete the chanting of three hundred thousand holy names, or in a year he would chant one hundred million names of Hari.

Some people consider that chanting the names of Krishna in a solitary place is in the category of "upamsu-japa," or "chanting very mildly." They say that this maha-mantra, or chanting the holy names of the Lord, should not be heard by others; only the person who is chanting should hear. If the lips move, or if the holy names are recited, then they will automatically be heard by others. But if such persons lack faith in the Vaisnavas who chant the holy names of the Lord, then by the influence of Kali they dare to quarrel with those Vaisnava chanters."

Descent of Lord Krishna as Sri Chaitanya Mahaprabhu

It's a great myth that Sri Chaitanya Mahaprabhu was only a great devotee of Lord Krishna but the populace is not aware that he was Lord Krishna himself who appeared in the form of a devotee. He is also known as prachanna or Gupta avatar means hidden incarnation of Lord Krishna who appeared as a devotee so that he can teach how the devotional service by way of Naam Sankirtan (Congregational chanting of the holy name) should be performed.

saṅkīrtana-pravartaka śrī-kṛṣṇa-caitanya
saṅkīrtana-yajñe tāṅre bhaje, sei dhanya

Lord Śrī Kṛṣṇa Caitanya is the initiator of saṅkīrtana [congregational chanting of the holy name of the Lord]. One who worships Him through saṅkīrtana is fortunate indeed.

(Chaitanya Charitramrita Adi lila 3.77)

Here are some of the scriptural references which clearly spell out that Sri Chaitanya Mahaprabhu is an incarnation of Lord Krishna. Mahabharata (Dana-dharma, Chapter 189 Vishnu-sahasra-nama-stotra)

suvarna-varno hemango varangas candanangadi
sannyasa-krc chamah santo nistha-santi-parayanah

'In His early pastimes He appears as a householder with a golden complexion. His limbs are beautiful, and His body, smeared with the pulp of sandalwood, seems like molten gold. In His later pastimes. He accepts the sannyasa order, and He is equipoised and peaceful. He is the highest abode of peace and devotion, for He silences the impersonalist non-devotees.'

कृष्णवर्णं त्विषाकृष्णं साङ्गोपाङ्गास्त्रपार्षद
यज्ञैः सङ्कीर्तनप्रायैर्यजन्ति हि सुमेधसः

In the Age of Kali, intelligent persons perform congregational chanting to worship the incarnation of Godhead who constantly sings the names of Kṛṣṇa. Although His complexion is not blackish, He is Kṛṣṇa Himself. He is accompanied by His associates, servants, weapons and confidential companions.

(Srimad Bhagavatam 11.5.32)

kalau yaṁ vidvaṁsaḥ sphuṭam abhiyajante dyuti-bharād
akṛṣṇāṅgaṁ kṛṣṇaṁ makha-vidhibhir utkīrtanamayaiḥ
upāsyaṁ ca prāhur yam akhila-caturthāśrama-juṣāṁ
sa devaś caitanyākṛtir atitarāṁ naḥ kṛpayatu

'By performing the sacrifice of congregational chanting of the holy name, scholars in the age of Kali worship Lord Krsna, who is now non-blackish because of the great upsurge of feelings of Srimati Radharani. He is the only worshipable Deity for the paramahamsas, who have attained the highest stage of the fourth order (sannyasa).

May that Supreme Personality of Godhead, Lord Caitanya, show us His great causeless mercy.'

(Dvitiya Sri Caitanyastakam, Stava mala of Srila Rupa Goswami)

In Upapuranas we hear Sri Krishna showing His mercy to Vedavyas by speaking to him as follows.

aham eva kvacid brahman
sannyāsāśramam āśritaḥ
hari-bhaktiṁ grāhayāmi
kalau pāpa-hatān narān

'O learned brāhmaṇa, sometimes I accept the renounced order of life to induce the fallen people of the Age of Kali to accept devotional service to the Lord.'

(Chaitanya Charitramrita Adi lila 3.83)

Apart from the above references there are many other references but it's difficult to put all the references in the book to maintain the brevity of same.

❑

Emperors Ruled Mathura

CHAPTER 3

Emperors Who Ruled Mathura

Some 5,000 years ago, under the rule of Sri Balaram and Sri Krishna Mathura was a well flourished city. Lord Krishna in due course became the king of Dwarka presently in Gujarat and his elder brother Shri Balramji became the king of Braja Mathura Mandal.

Archaeological excavations by Archaeological Survey of India (ASI) and in the opinion of various historians, Mathura was a center of learning under different civilizations. It is also a important center of trade due to its location where the northern trade route of the Indo-Gangetic Plain met with the routes to Malwa (central India) and the west coast. Archaeologists have discovered a fragment of Mathura red sandstone from Rakhigarhi, a site of Indus Valley civilization dated to 3rd millennium BCE which was used as a grindstone which was also a popular material for historic period sculptures.

Mathura was the capital of the Surasena Kingdom. In the later period, the city was ruled under the Maurya empire. Megasthenes, writing of the early 3rd century BCE, mentions Mathura as a great city under the name Μέθορα (Méthora).

Mathura came under Indo-Greek control some time between 180 BCE and 100 BCE, and remained so as late as 70 BCE according to the Yavanarajya inscription, which was found in Maghera, a town 17 kilometres (11 mi) from Mathura. The opening of the 3 line text of this inscription in Brahmi script translates as: ***"In the 116th year of the Yavana kingdom..."*** or ***"In the 116th year of Yavana hegemony" ("Yavanarajya")***.

- Under the region of Kushanas, art and culture flourished and took new heights and is now famously known as the Mathura School of Art. Mathura came under the control of Mahakshatrapa Sodasa, but even after this several of his successors ruled as Kushans' vassals, paid allegiance to the Kushans in an inscription at Sarnath, dating to the 3rd year of the reign of the Kushan emperor Kanishka the Great 130 CE. Artielers of Mathura were most active during the epoch of the great Kushan emperors Kanishka,

Huvishka, Vasudeva whose reign represents the Golden Age of Mathura sculpture.

- Under the rule of Chandragupta Vikramaditya, a marvelous and magnificient of Bhagwan Vishnu was built at the site of Katra Keshavadeva, presently the disputed site of Shahi Idgah Mosque. Kalidasa one of the greatest Sanskrit poets who took shelter of Shri Haridas Community in Vrindavan. Who also had glorified the groves of Vrindavan and Govardhan hill as:

"...the king of Mathura, whose fame was acknowledged in song even by the devatas... At that moment, though still in Mathura, it appears as if Ganga has merged with Yamuna at the Sangam... In a Vrindavan garden which is superior even to Kubera's garden, known as Chaitra-ratha... You can, as well, during rains, look at the dancing peacocks, while sitting in a pleasant cave of the Goverdhan Mountain"

Buddhist Chinese Monk *Faxian*(Fa hien) who travelled to India at the age of 65 mentions about Mathura city as a center of Buddhism in 399 CE. He found that people use to follow the regulative principles of Dharma where people did not even kill animals, no one consumed wine, and did not eat onion or garlic. People were so pious that they provide visiting saints and priests with accommodation, food and clothes to perform scholarly works.

Xuanzang, a Chinese Buddhist monk who visited India during the 7th Century mentions the city of Mathura as Mot'ulo. He had recorded that there are 3 stupas built by King Ashoka, there are also about 20 sangharamas with 2,000 priests and 5 deva temples in which sectaries of all kinds live.

The famous female *Alvar* saint, *Andal* the daughter of Periyalvar who was monk the 12 Alvar saints had visualized Vraj Yatra starting from Mathura then proceeded to Gokul, the Yamuna, Vrindavan, Govardhan, and finished at Dwarka.

Islamic Invasions

On December, 2 1018 invaders descended upon the fort of Mahavan on the outskirts of the city of Mathura. King Kulchand fought valiantly but the forces of Mahmud became victorious. Approximately 5,000-50,000 Hindus were killed drowned or became the prey of crocodiles.

It is described by the historian al-Utbi (Abu Nasr Muhammad bin Muhammad al Jabbaru-al-'Utbi) in his work Tarikh Yamini as follows:-

''In the middle of the city there was a temple larger and firmer than the rest, which can neither be described nor painted. It was the legendary temple of Vasudeva. Mahmud wrote: ***"If any should wish to construct a building equal to this, he would not be able to do it without expending a hundred thousand thousand***

(100 million) red dinars, and it would occupy 200 years, even though the most experienced and able workmen were employed."

Among the idols there were five made of gold, each 15 feet tall, fixed in the air without support. In the eyes of one of these idols there were two rubies, of such value, that if any one were to sell such as are like them, he would obtain 50,000 dinars. The temple which Mahmud Ghazni was so amazed by was Katra Keshavdeva (Krishna Janmabhoomi temple).

On another, there was a sapphire purer than water, and more sparkling than crystal; the weight was 450 miskals (1 miskal = 4.5 grams). The two feet of another idol weighed 4,400 miskals, and the entire quantity of gold yielded by the bodies of these idols, was 98,300 miskals – that's 442 kilos of pure gold. There were also 200 silver idols, but they could not be weighed without breaking them to pieces and putting them into scales.

German Indologist Mr. Anton Fuhrer, who worked with the Archaeological Survey of India, recorded the foundations of a temple dedicated to Vishnu at the Katra site:

"Jajja, who carried the burden of the varga, together with a committee of trustees (goshtijana), built a large temple of Vishnu, brilliantly white and touching the clouds."

Jajja was a vassal of the Gahadavalas in charge of Mathura, and the committee mentioned in the prasasti could have been of an earlier Vaishnava temple. The temple built by Jajja at Katra was destroyed by the forces of Qutubuddin Aibak, though Feroz Tughlaq (r. 1351-88 CE) was also said to have attacked it. It was repaired and survived till the reign of Sikandar Lodi.

In the twelfth century, Bhatta Lakshmidhara, chief minister of the Gahadavala King Govindachandra wrote the earliest surviving collection of verses in praise of the sacred sites of Mathura in his work Krtyakalpataru, which has been described as ***"the first re- statement of the theory of Tirtha-yatra (pilgrimage)".*** In his Krtyakalpataru, Bhatta Lakshmidhara devoted an enitre section (9) to Mathura.

In the later years the city of Mathura was sacked again by Sikandar Lodi, who ruled the Sultanate of Delhi from 1489 to 1517 CE. Sikandar Lodi earned the epithet of 'Butt Shikan', the 'Destroyer of Idols'.

Ferishta recorded that Sikandar Lodi was a staunch Muslim, with a passion for vandalizing heathen temples:

"He was firmly attached to the Muhmaaden religion, and made a point of destroying all Hindu temples. In the city of Mathura he caused masjids and bazaars to be built opposite the bathing-stairs leading to the river, and ordered that no Hindus should be allowed to bath there. He forbade the barbers to shave the beards and heads of the inhabitants of Mathura, in order to prevent the Hindus following their usual practices at such pilgrimages."

In Tarikh-i Daudi, of 'Abdu-lla (written during the time of Jahangir) said of Sikandar Lodi:

"Sikandar Lodi was very zealous as a Musalman that he utterly destroyed diverse places of worship of the infidels, and left not a vestige remaining of them. He entirely ruined the shrines of Mathura, the mine of heathenism, and turned their principal Hindu places of worship into caravanserais and colleges. Their stone images were given to the butchers to serve them as meat-weights, and all the Hindus in Mathura were strictly prohibited from shaving their heads and beards, and performing their ablutions. He thus put an end to all the idolatrous rites of the infidels there; and no Hindu, if he wished to have his head or beard shaved, could get a barber to do it. Every city thus conformed as he desired to the customs of Islam."

Sri Vallabhacharya ji and Lord Shri Chaitanya Mahaprabhu arrived in the Braj region, in search of sacred places that had been destroyed or lost. In Shrikrsnashrayah strotram, that makes up the Sodashagrantha, Vallabha said of his age:

"The Malechchhas (demoniac nature/one who doesn't follow scriptures in this context) have surrounded all the holy places with the result that they have become infected with evil.

Besides, the holy people are full of sorrow. At such a time Krishna alone is my way."

The Portuguese, Father Antonio Monserrate (1536 CE-1600 CE), who was on a Jesuit mission at the Mughal

Court during the times of Akbar, visited Mathura in 1580-82, and noted that all temples built at sites associated with the deeds of Krishna were in ruins:-

"It (Mathura) used to be a great and well-populated city, with splendid buildings and a great circuit of walls. The ruins plainly indicate how imposing its buildings were. For out of these forgotten ruins, were dug up columns and very ancient statues, of skillful and cunning workmanship. Only one Hindu temple is left out of many; for the Musalmans have completely destroyed all except the pyramids. Huge crowds of pilgrims come from all over India to this temple, which is situated on the high bank of the Jomanis (Yamuna)."

The Katra Keshavadeva temple was rebuilt by the Bundela Rajah Vir Singh Deo at a cost of thirty-three lakh rupees when the gold was priced at around Rs.10/- per tola. And the grand structure of the temple in Mathura was regarded a ***"wonder of the age"***.

The Mughal Emperor Aurangzeb, demolished Shri Krishna Janmabhoomi a Hindu temple on the remains of which he built the Shahi-Eidgah Mosque during his rule, that why the present day Sri Krishna Janmabhoomi temple which we see is at a far height than the walking pathway. Mathura's name was changed to Islamabad. In 1669, Aurangzeb issued a general order for the demolition of Hindu schools and temples, in 1670, specifically ordered the destruction of the Keshavadeva temple was issued. Saqi Mustaid Khan recorded:

"On Thursday, 27th January/15 Ramzan (27 January 1670)... the Emperor as the promoter of justice and overthrower of mischief, as a knower of truth and destroyer of oppression as the zephyr of the garden of victory and the reviver of the faith of the Prophet, issued orders for the demolition of the temple situated in Mathura, famous as the Dehra of Kesho Rai. In a short time by the great exertions of his officers, the destruction of this strong foundation of infidelity was accomplished and on its site a lofty mosque was built by the expenditure of a large sum... Praised be the august God of the faith of Islam, that in the auspicious reign of this destroyer of infidelity and turbulence, such a wonderful and seemingly impossible work was successfully accomplished.

On seeing this instance of the strength of the emperor's faith and the grandeur of his devotion to God, the proud Rajas were stifled, and in amazement they stood like images facing the wall. The idols, large and small, set with costly jewels, which had been set up in the temple, were brought to Agra, and buried under the step of the mosque of the Begum Shahib in order to be continuously trodden upon. The name of Mathura was changed to Islamabad."

The barbaric conquest by the Muslim rulers led to the destruction of all Hindu (including Buddhist and Jain) temples and monuments in and around Mathura.

Buddhism, facing decline, never revived, where as the Jains and Hindus were unable to erect any temples that were not sooner or later demolished for the next 400 years.

Many of the sites that had been places of religious importance were abandoned and gradually sank beneath the earth. This entails that the fresh excavation should be undertaken by the Archaeological Survey of India. On a conversation with an officer of ASI, I came to know the fact that many people excavated on their own in the greed of finding valuable articles which damaged much heritage in and around Braj mandal. But some of them were not forgotten, owing to the persistence of oral tradition, the refashioning of a temple into a mosque, or the presence of humble shrines.

According the biographer of Raja Jai Singh, Atmaram, when Jai Singh was campaigning against the Jat Raja Churaman Singh, he bathed at Radha Kund on the full moon of Kartik, went to Mathura in the month of Shravan in 1724, and performed the marriage of his daughter on Janmashtami. He then undertook a pilgrimage of the 12 sacred forests of Braj, and, on his return to Mathura, founded religious establisments, and celebrated Holi.

During the reign and expansion of Maratha Empire, pilgrimage to the holy places in the north became quite frequent. Pilgrims required protection on the way so they took advantage of the constant movement of troops that journeyed to and back from their homeland for military purposes. That is how the practice arose of ladies accompanying military expeditions. The mother of Peshwa Balaji Baji Rao, Kashitai performed her famous pilgrimage for four years in the north, visiting Mathura, Prayag, Ayodhya, Banaras, and other holy places.

Images of various Firmans issued by Aurangzeb:

Firman issued by Aurangzeb to convert Hindus. ₹ 4 to a Hindu male, ₹ 2 to a female. Dated: 7 April 1685.

If Devi Chand, Zamindar of Manoharpur, who's in prison, becomes Muslim, better for him. Else he be killed.

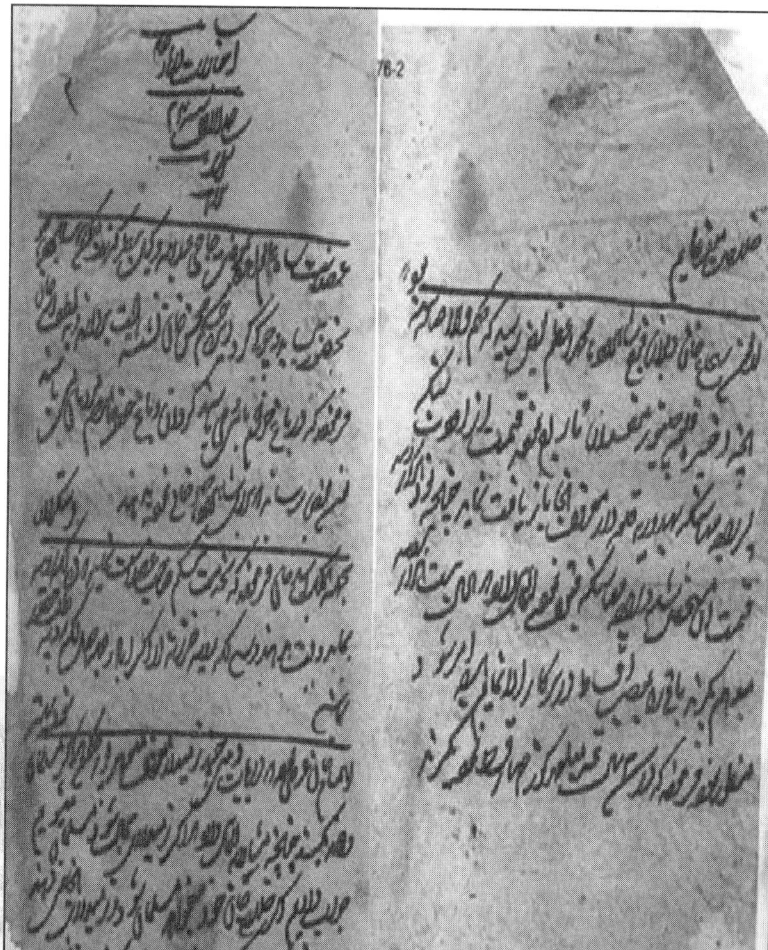

Shaikh Abdul Momin, Faujdar of Bithur, wrote he had converted 150 Hindus and had given them saropas and cash.

Aurangzeb's order for demolishing the temple at Goner (Amber) Siyaha Akhbarat-i- Darbar-i-Mu'alla Julus, 28 Mar 1686.

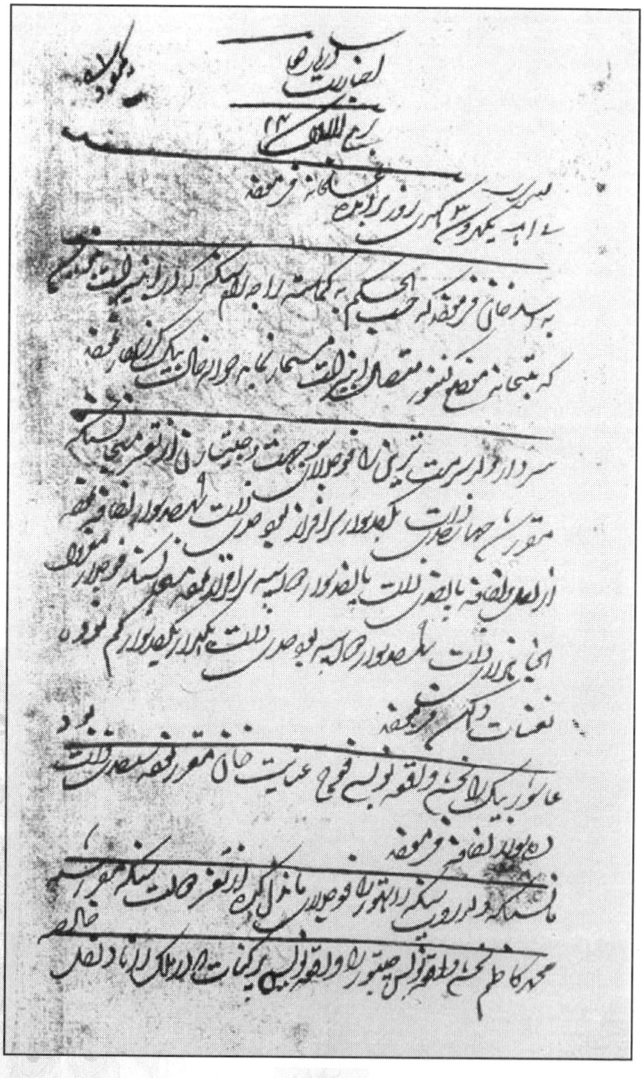

Demolition of Bindu-Madhav Temple at Banaras. Siyah Akhbarat-i- Darbar-i- Mu'alla Julus 26, Ramzan 20 / 13 Sep 1682.

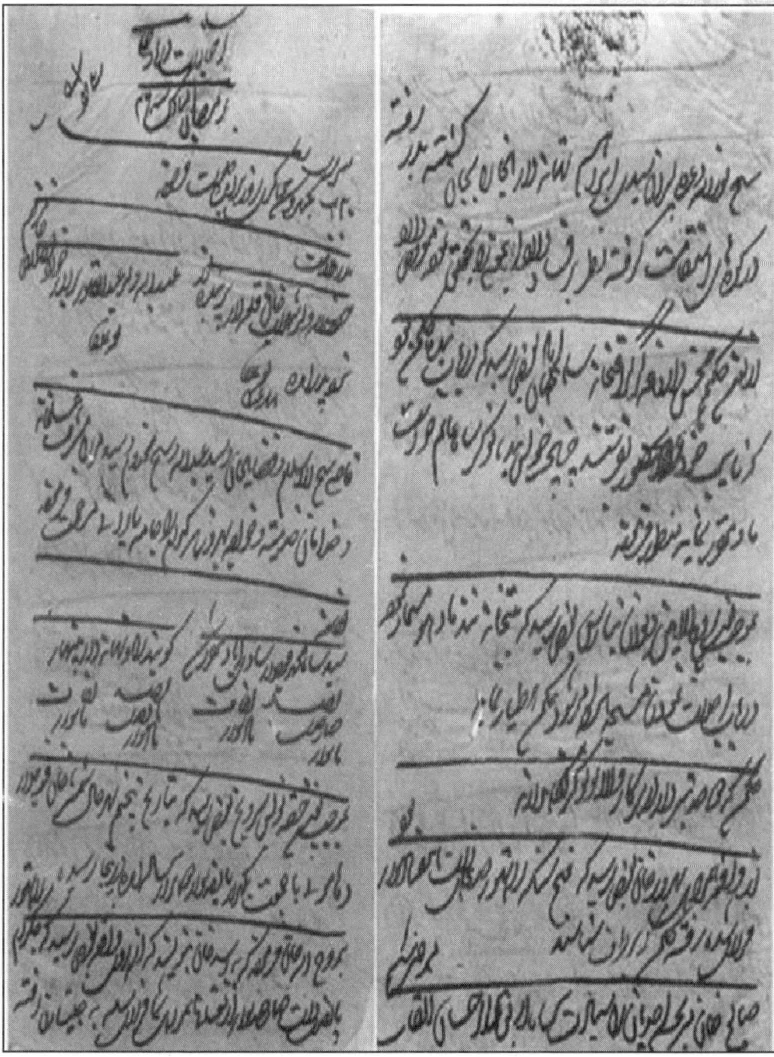

Orders to Jawahar Chand, Daroga of the beldars, that whichever temples come in the way of the Emperor be demolished.

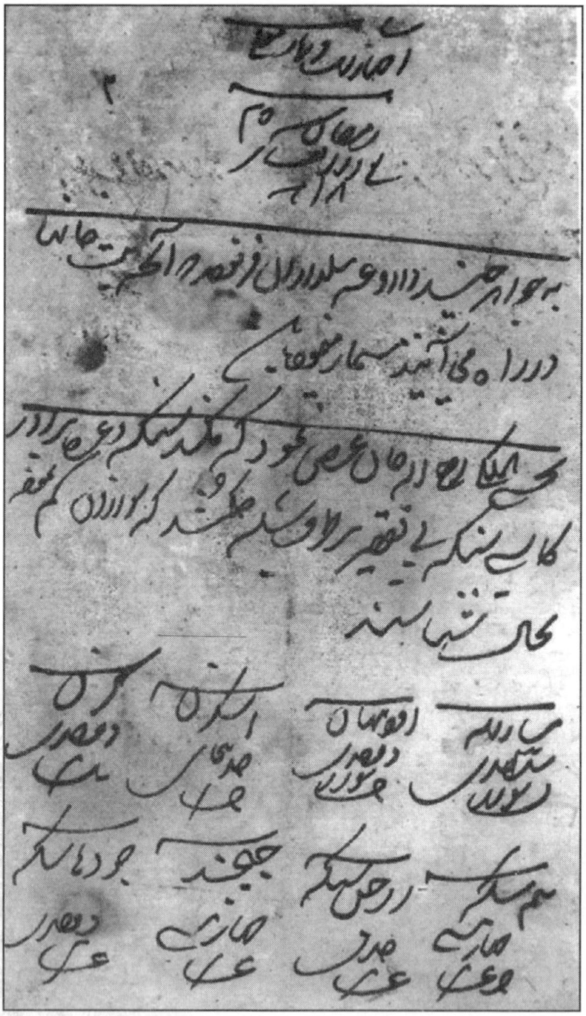

Orders for demolition of Jagannath Temple, Orissa Siyah Akhbarat-i- Darbar-i-Mu'alla Julus 24, Jamadi I, 23 / 01 Jun 1681.

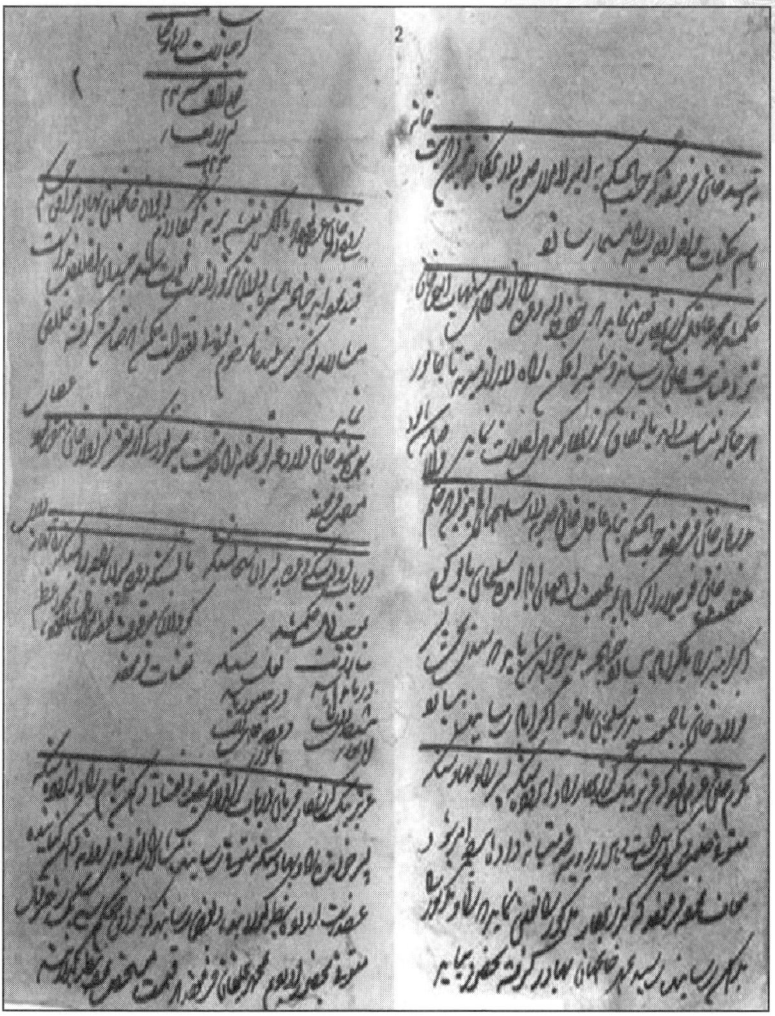

Orders for the destruction of temples on the bank of Maharana's Lake, Udaipur. 23rd December 1679.

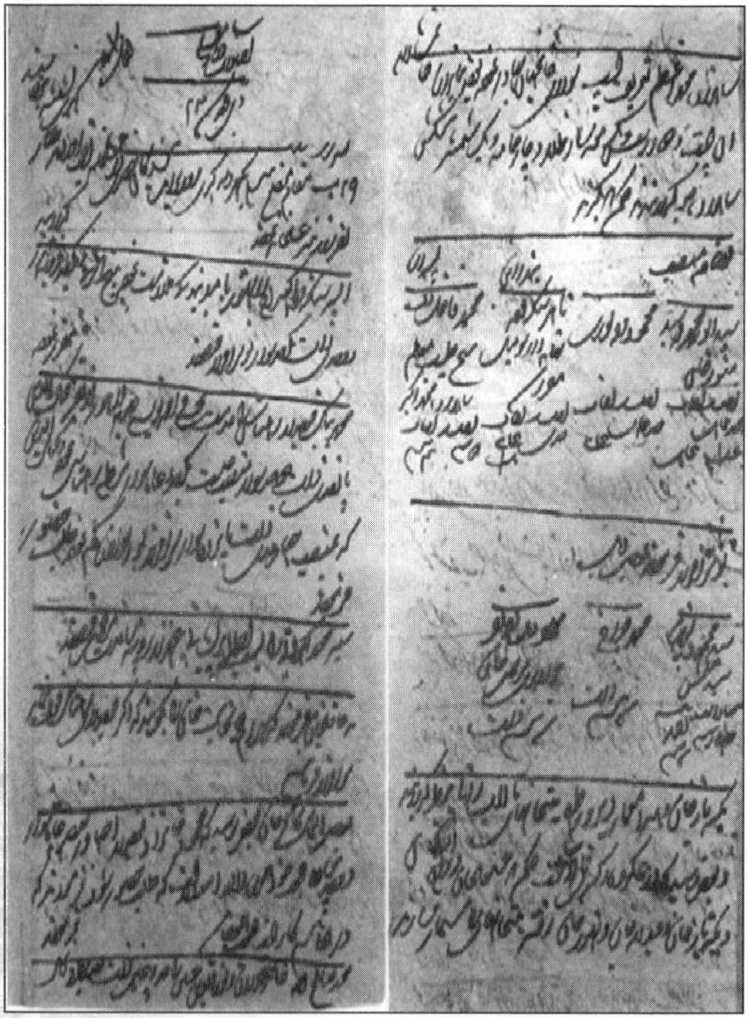

Demolition of Kalka's Temple near Delhi - I. Siyah Waqa'i- Darbar Regnal Year 10, Rabi I, 23/ 3 Sep 1667.

General Order by Aurangzeb for the Destruction of Temples. (9th April 1669)

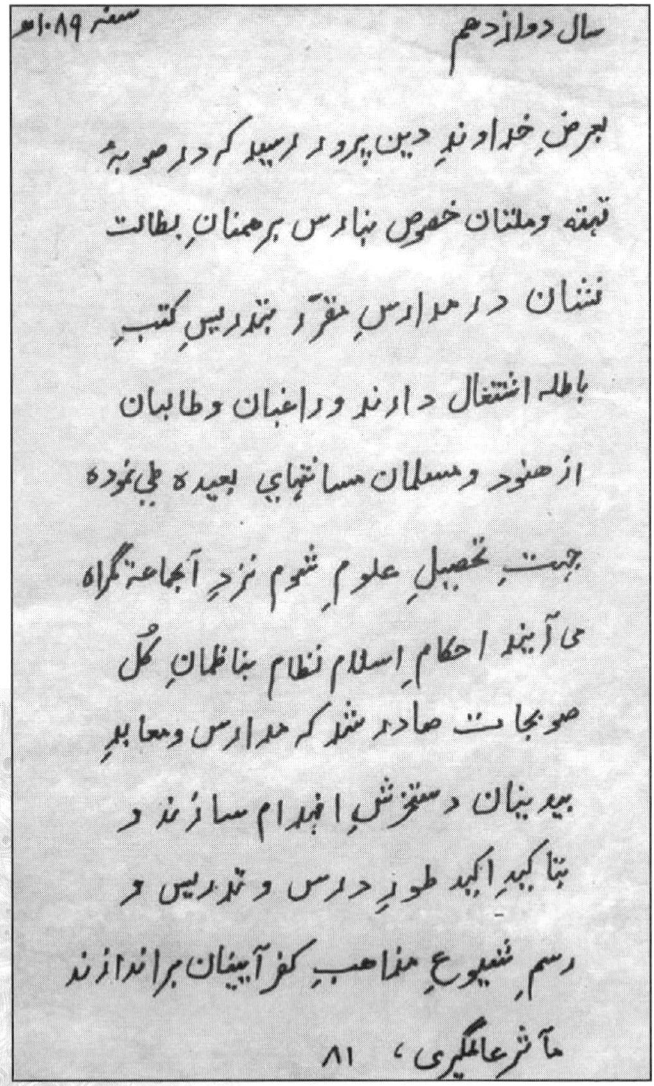

سال دوازدهم　　　　صفر ۱۰۸۹ھ

بعرض خداوند دین پرور رسید که در صوبهٔ
تهته وملتان خصوص بنارس برهمنان بطالت
نشان در مدارس مقرر بتدریس کتب
باطله اشتغال دارند وراغبان وطالبان
از هنود ومسلمان مسافتهای بعیده طی نموده
جهت تحصیل علوم شوم نزد آن جماعهٔ گمراه
می آیند احکام اسلام نظام بناظمان کل
صوبجات صادر شد که مدارس ومعابد
بی دینان دستخوش انهدام سازند و
بتاکید اکید طور درس و تدریس و
رسم شیوع مذاهب کفر آیینان براندازند
مآثر عالمگیری، ۸۱

Demolition of Kalka's Temple near Delhi - I. Siyah Waqa'i- Darbar Regnal Year 10, Rabi I, 23/ 3 Sep 1667.

امورات حضور کشور
کشای ماه ربیع الثانی
سنه ۹ جلوس بیست ۲۳ منه

بعرض حضرت رسید که در متهراجیو در بتخانه که کیشوداس
جیو یک کتهره سنگی بی شکوه نموده است حضرت شنیده
فرمودند که در مذهب مسلمانی بتخانه را دیدن هم خوب نیست و
این بی شکوه در آن کتهره راست کنانیده این سخن مسلمانان را
خوب نیست از این ممر این کتهره را دور باید نمود به عبدالنبی
خان فرمودند که شما رفته آن کتهره را از میان آن بتخانه دور
نمایند آن زمان عبدالنبی خان آمده آن کتهره دور کرده
بعد پیش بادشاه جیو رفته معلوم نمود که آن کتهره را از
میان آن بتخانه دور کرده در آن کوتهری که سری کیسوداس
جیو می نشستند بیرون آن کوتهری در جنگ چوبین آن کتهره
سنگین دارا شکوه کنانیده بود تمام خلق متصل آن کتهره را دور
نمودند سابق در آنجا کتهره چوبین بود عبدالنبی خان گفت آن
کتهره سابق چوبین را آورده ایستاده بکنند آن زمان همگان
کتهره چوب را ایستاده کرد آن روز بلوه هم متهراجیو بود
بعد از آن ایستاده نموده کتهره چوب جمله خلق در شن نمود.

Demolition of the Temple of Vishwanath (Banaras). August 1669 A.D.

It was reported that, ***"according to the Emperor's command, his officers had demolished the Temple of Vishwanath at Kashi."*** (Maasir- i-'Alamgiri, p. 88)

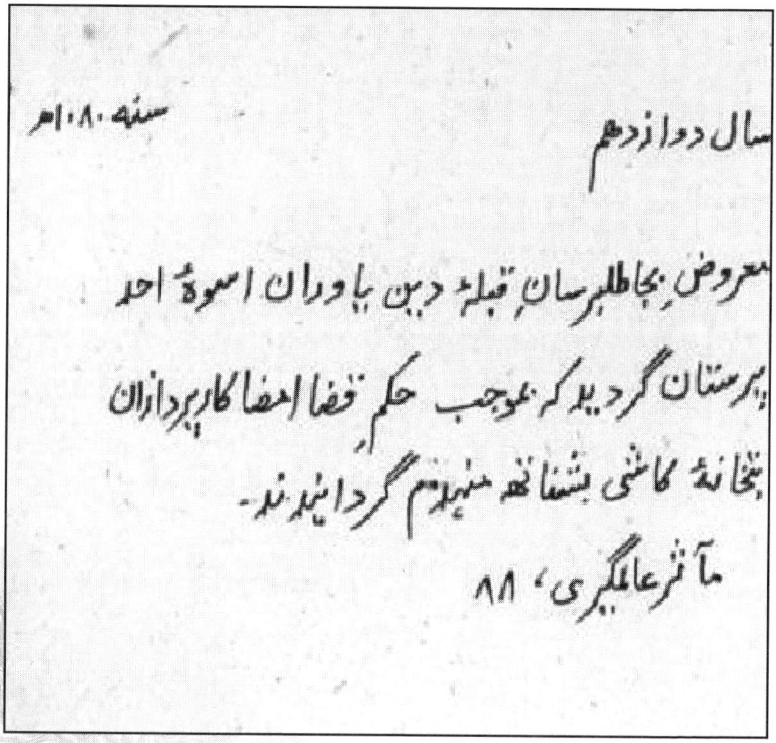

سنه ۱۰۸۰ھ

سال دوازدهم

معروض بجا طلبرسان قبلهٔ دین باوران اسوهٔ احد

پرستان گردید کہ بموجب حکم قضا امضا کارپردازان

بتخانۂ کاشی بشنانهه منہدم گردانیدند۔

مآثر عالمگیری، ۸۸

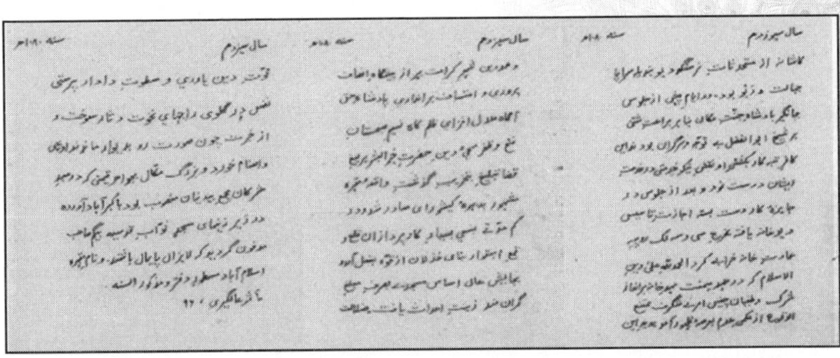

Firman by Aurangzeb in 1670 to demolish Krishna Temple of Mathura and bury the deities under stairs of Begum Sahiba Masjid (situated in Agra)

❑

धर्म = पंथ ???

CHAPTER 4

Dharma Vs Pantha

Dharma

Dharma in simple terms is Nature or one's constitutional position. For example, the nature of fire is to give heat and light without it we can't know it is fire. Similarly, we all are souls and not this body which is part and parcel of super soul. As a part it's our duty to serve the whole i.e., as a soul we need to primarily love and serve the supersoul.

Just as 'Dharma is that which accomplishes the three tasks of keeping the setup of the society in excellent condition, bringing about the worldly progress of every living being, and facilitating their progress in the spiritual realm as well.' We understand from this definition the vastness of Dharma and its extraordinary importance in human life.

In the context of a Nation, Dharma is its life. Therefore, only if the lifestyle of the society is based upon Dharma, the Nation will become prosperous and immortal. A Nation that is devoid of the foundation of Dharma will, in time, face destruction.

Just as there is no life without respiration, so also life without Dharma is not a worthy life, as it amounts to an existence like animals. Strict Adherence to Dharma is the only way by which a human is differentiated from animals. Dharma is not for developing intelligence; it is for developing character and wisdom.

धर्मं तु साक्षाद्भगवत्प्रणीतं
न वै विदुॠर्षयो नापि देवा।
न सिद्धमुख्या असुरा मनुष्या:
कुतो नु विद्याधरचारणादय: ॥ १९ ॥

Real religious principles are enacted by the Supreme Personality of Godhead. Although fully situated in the mode of goodness, even the great ṛṣis who occupy the topmost planets cannot ascertain the real religious principles, nor can the demigods or the leaders of Siddhaloka, to say nothing of the asuras, ordinary human beings, Vidyādharas and Cāraṇas.

(Srimad Bhagvatam 6.3.19)

आगमानां हि सर्वेषाम् आचारः श्रेष्ठ उच्यते ।
आचारप्रभवो धर्मो धर्मादायुर्विवर्धते ।।

When compared with all knowledge, good conduct is considered to be superior; because Dharma is based on achars (Conduct conforming to Shruti and Smruti). When man abides by Achardharma (Code of righteous conduct), his life is prolonged. **(Mahabharat, Anushasanparva, Adhyaya 107, Shloka 147)**

धर्मादर्थः प्रभवति धर्मात्प्रभवते सुखम् ।
धर्मेण लभतेसर्वंधर्मसारमिदं जगत् ।।

Dharma bestows wealth and happiness. In fact, everything can be obtained through Dharma. This entire universe sustains itself on the foundation of Dharma.

(Valmikiramayan, Aranyakanḍa, Sarga 8, Shloka 26)

ऊर्ध्वबाहुर्विरौम्येष न च कश्चिच्छृणोति मे ।
धर्मादर्थश्चकामश्च स किमर्थं न सेव्यते ।।

(Sage Vyas says) With my arms raised, I am mourning, yet no one listens to me. (O human beings) Dharma accomplishes both, earning of wealth and fulfilling of desires. Then, why do you not abide by Dharma?

(Mahabharat, Swargarohanparva, Adhyaya 5, Shloka 46)

सुखस्य मूलं धर्मः । धर्मस्य मूलमर्थः ।
अर्थस्य मूलं राज्यम् । राज्यमूलम् इन्द्रियजयः ।
इन्द्रियजयस्य मूलं विनयः । विनयस्य मूलं वृद्धोपसेवा।
वृद्धोपसेवया विज्ञानम् । विज्ञानेन आत्मानं सम्पादयेत् ।
सम्पादितात्मा जितात्मा भवति ।

Origin of happiness lies in following Dharma. Origin of Dharma is in earning wealth by righteous means which, in turn, helps in securing a kingdom. Humbleness is essential for gaining control over the sense organs and the mind. For achieving humbleness, it is essential to serve those who are rich in knowledge. Service unto such individuals helps acquire knowledge about the soul, leading to self-realisation.

(Chanakyasutra, Adhyaya 1, Sutra 1-9)

स्वल्पमप्यस्य धर्मस्य त्रायते महतो भयात् ।

Even if Dharma is followed to a small extent, it protects one from largest danger.

(Shrimadbhagwadgita Adhyaya 2, Shloka 40)

अधम एव मूलं सर्वरोगाणाम् ।

Disobedience to the word of Supreme Personality of Godhead is the root cause of all diseases. There are three categories of miseries, namely Adhibhoutik, Adhidaivik and Adhyatmik. Adhibhoutik diseases arise from other living entities such as mosquito biting, slap by someone. Adhidaivik diseases occur due to malefic planets, curses of Saints and Sages and wrath of Deities etc. such as earthquakes, famines other natural calamities.

Adhyatmik diseases are distress due to one's own physical body or mind such as distress, pain of body.

Panth

The word pantha in simple terms means way path.

All other path which was enunciated by the humans i.e., other than by God himself by whatever name called are known as pantha. As there is only one Dharma that is Sanatana Dharma. Hinduism including Sikhism, Buddhism, Jainism are part of it. Any other pathway claiming to be religion is strictly a pantha which is not an eternal dharma as dharma means which is eternal but pantha which is a temporary religion.

Breaking of Idols in Islam

In the past few years some of the world heritage sites have been destroyed which is a great loss to heritage which the new generation can know about. Some of them are:-

- **ISIS militants destroy 2,000-year-old statue of lion at Palmyra**

Islamic State jihadis have destroyed a 2,000-year-old statue of a lion outside the museum in the Syrian city of Palmyra, the country's antiquities director has said.

Maamoun Abdelkarim said the statue, known as the Lion of Al-lāt, was an irreplaceable piece. ***"ISIS members destroyed the Lion of Al-lāt, which is a unique piece that is three meters [10 ft] tall and weighs 15 tonnes,"*** Abdelkarim told AFP. ***"It's the most serious crime they have committed against Palmyra's heritage."***

The limestone statue was discovered in 1977 by a Polish archaeological mission at the temple of Al-lāt, a pre-Islamic Arabian goddess, and dated back to the 1st century BC.

- **Destruction of Bamiyan Buddha**

The 2001 destruction of the two giant Buddhas in Bamiyan is, by far, the most spectacular attack against the historical and cultural heritage of Afghanistan committed during the country's recent period of turmoil.

On February 26, 2001, and after having consulted a college of 'ulama', Mullah Muhammad Omar, the leader of the Taliban, issued a decree ordering the elimination of all non-Islamic statues and sanctuaries in Afghanistan. A kind of jihad was launched against the two Buddhas — the one to the east 38 meters high, and the other to the west, 55 meters high — hewn into the cliff of Bamiyan. ***"Our soldiers are working hard; they are using all available arms against them,"*** said the Taliban's spokesman. Rockets and tank shells were brought in to help, and the destruction was completed with dynamite. On March 14, the Taliban issued a public announcement that the giant figures had been destroyed.

- **Conversion of Hagia Sophia into Mosque**

  The world-famous Hagia Sophia museum in Istanbul - originally founded as a cathedral - has been turned back into a mosque.

  Turkey's President Recep Tayyip Erdogan announced the decision after a court annulled the site's museum status.

  Built 1,500 years ago as an Orthodox Christian cathedral, Hagia Sophia was converted into a mosque after the Ottoman conquest in 1453.

  In 1934 it became a museum and is now a UNESCO World Heritage site.

  Islamists in Turkey long called for it to be converted to a mosque but secular opposition members opposed the move. The proposal prompted criticism from religious and political leaders worldwide. Defending the decision, President Erdogan stressed that the country had exercised its sovereign right in converting it back to a mosque.

Interior view of the Hagia Sophia, showing Christian and Islamic elements on the main dome and pendentives.

The destruction of above mentioned two heritage sites and conversion of a age old church into mosque were of recent years whereas if we go in the past era the list of such acts are very long which cannot be included in a single book.

Is it obligatory to destroy statues in Islam, even if they are part of the legacy of human civilization? Why is it that when the Sahaabah conquered other lands and saw statues there they did not destroy them?

The evidence of sharee'ah indicates that it is obligatory to destroy idols, for example:

- Muslim (969) narrated that Abu'l-Hayaaj al-Asadi said: 'Ali ibn Abi Taalib said to me: ***"Shall I not send you with the same instructions as the Messenger of Allaah (peace and blessings of Allaah be upon him) sent me? 'Do not leave any image without defacing it or any built-up grave without leveling it.'"***
- Muslim (832) narrated from 'Urwah ibn 'Abasah that he said to the Prophet (peace and blessings of Allaah be upon him): ***"With what were you sent?" He said, "I was sent to uphold the ties of kinship, to break the idols, and so that Allaah would be worshipped alone with no partner or associate."***

The obligation to destroy them is even stronger if they are worshipped instead of Allaah.

- Al-Bukhaari (3020) and Muslim (2476) narrated that

Jareer ibn 'Abd-Allaah al-Bajali said: The Messenger of Allaah (peace and blessings of Allaah be upon him) said to me: ***"O Jareer, will you not relieve me of Dhu'l-Khalsah?"*** That was a house (in Yemen) belonging to the (tribe of) Khath'am, which was called Ka'bat al- Yamaaniyyah. I set out with one hundred and fifty horsemen. I used not to sit firm on horses and I mentioned that to the Messenger of Allaah (peace and blessings of Allaah be upon him).

He struck me on my chest with his hand and said, 'O Allaah! Make him firm and make him one who guides others and is guided on the right path.' So Jareer went and burned it with fire, then Jareer sent a man called Abu Artaat to the Messenger of Allaah (peace and blessings of Allaah be upon him). He said, ***"I did not come to you until we had left it like a scabby camel."*** Then the Messenger of Allaah (peace and blessings of Allaah be upon him) blessed the horses of (the tribe of) Ahmas and their men five times.

Al-Haafiz Ibn Hajar said

This hadeeth indicates that it is prescribed to remove things that may tempt or confuse the people, whether they are buildings, people, animals or inanimate objects.

- The Prophet (peace and blessings of Allaah be upon him) sent Khaalid ibn al-Waleed (may Allaah be pleased with him) on a campaign to destroy al-'Uzza. and he sent Sa'd ibn Zayd al-Ashhali (may Allaah be pleased with him) on a campaign to destroy Manaat.

- And he sent 'Amr ibn al-'Aas (may Allaah be pleased with him) on a campaign to destroy Suwaa'. All of that happened after the Conquest of Makkah.

  Al-Bidaayah wa'l-Nihaayah, 4/712.776.5/83; al-Seerah al-Nabawiyyah by Dr. 'Ali al-Salaabi, 2/1186.

  Al-Nawawi said in Sharh Muslim when discussing the issue of image-making:

  They were unanimously agreed that whatever casts a shadow is not allowed and must be changed.

  Images that cast a shadow are three-dimensional images like these statues.

With regard to what is said about the Sahaabah (may Allaah be pleased with them) not destroying idols in the conquered lands, this is merely conjecture. The companions of the Prophet (peace and blessings of Allaah be upon him) would not have left idols and statues alone, especially since they were worshipped at that time.

If it is asked, how come the Sahaabah left alone the ancient idols of the Pharaohs and Phoenicians? The answer is that these idols fall into one of three categories:

- These idols may have been in remote places that the Sahaabah did not reach; when the Sahaabah conquered Egypt, for example, that does not mean that they reached every part of the land.
- These idols may not have been visible, rather they may have been inside Pharaonic buildings etc. The

Prophet (peace and blessings of Allaah be upon him) told us to hasten when passing through the abodes of the wrongdoers and those who had been punished, and he forbade entering such places. In al-Saheehayn it says: ***"Do not enter upon those who have been punished unless you are weeping, lest there befall you something like that which befall them."*** He (peace and blessings of Allaah be upon him) said that when he passed by ashaab al-hijr [the dwellers of the rocky tract – see al-Hijr 15:80], in the land of Thamood, the people of Saalih (peace be upon him).

According to another report narrated in al-Saheehayn, ***"If you are not weeping, then do not enter upon them, lest there befall you something like that which befall them."***

What we think is that if the companions of the Prophet (peace and blessings of Allaah be upon him) saw a temple or building belonging of these people, they did not enter it or even look at what was inside it.

This will dispel any confusion about why the Sahaabah did not see the Pyramids or what is inside them. There is also the possibility that their doors and entrances were covered with sand at that time.

- Many of these idols that are visible nowadays were covered and hidden, and have only been discovered recently, or they have been brought from remote places that the companions of the Prophet (peace and blessings of Allaah be upon him) did not reach.

Al-Zarkali was asked about the Pyramids and the Sphinx etc: Did the Sahaabah who entered Egypt see them?

He said: They were mostly covered with sand, especially the Sphinx. Shibh Jazeerat al-'Arab, 4/1188.

Then even if we assume that there was a statue that was visible and not hidden, then we still have to prove that the Sahaabah saw it and were able to destroy it.

The fact of the matter is that the Sahaabah (may Allaah be pleased with them) would not have been able to destroy some of these statues. It took twenty days to destroy some of these statues even with tools, equipment, and explosives etc., that were not available to the Sahaabah at all.

This is indicated by what Ibn Khuldoon said in al-Muqaddimah (p. 383), that the caliph al-Rasheed was unable to destroy the estrade of Chosroes. He started to do that, and he gathered men and tools, and burned it with fire, and poured vinegar on it, but he was unable to do it. And the caliph al-Ma'moon wanted to destroy the Pyramids in Egypt and he gathered workers but he could not do it.

With regard to the excuse that these statues are part of the legacy of mankind, no attention should be paid to such words. Al-Laat, al-'Uzaa, Hubal, Manaat and other idols were also a legacy for those who worshipped them among Quraysh and the Arabs.

This is a legacy, but it is a haraam legacy which should be uprooted. When the command comes from Allaah and His Messenger, then the believer must hasten to obey, and the command of Allaah and His Messenger cannot be rejected on the grounds of this flimsy excuse.

Source:

https://islamqa.info/en/answers/20894/obligation-to-destroy-idols

Excerpts from Quran

The Quran relates how Ibrahim (AS) waged war against the idols, which were worshipped in his time. Ibrahim (AS) called his people in Mesopotamia to worship Allaah alone and to stop worshipping the idols, which could neither bring them benefit nor cause harm to them. He wanted to free his people from idol-worship and rid them of myths and legends. He asked his people about these idols, as Allaah tells us (interpretation of the meaning):

"And recite to them the story of Ibrahim (Abraham). When he said to his father and his people: 'What do you worship?' They said: 'We worship idols, and to them we are ever devoted.' He said: "Do they hear you, when you call on (them)? Or do they benefit you or do they harm (you)?' They said: '(Nay) but we found our fathers doing so'" [Quran 26: 69-74].

The part of the story which is directly relevant in the context of this discussion is the determination of Ibrahim (AS) to destroy these idols, as is related in the Quran:

"And by Allah, I will certainly plan against your idols - after you go away and turn your backs" [Quran 22: 57]

And then he broke the idols:

"Then he cast a glance at the stars, And he said: 'Verily, I am sick (with plague). [He did this trick to remain in their temple of idols to destroy them and not to accompany them to the pagan feast)].' So they turned away from him, and departed (for fear of the disease). Then he turned to their aalihah (gods) and said: 'Will you not eat (of the offering before you)? What is the matter with you that you speak not?' Then he turned upon them, striking (them) with (his) right hand" [Quran 37: 93]

Ibrahim (AS) broke all the idols except the biggest one, which he left so that his people could ask it who had destroyed the others (they would then realise how foolish they had been, when they would see that it obviously couldn't speak let alone answer them):

So he broke them to pieces, (all) except the biggest of them, that they might turn to it" [Quran 21:58].

Just as Allaah commanded Ibrahim (AS) to destroy the idols, He also commanded the Prophet Muhammad (SAWS) to do the same.

Years after the demise of Ibrahim (AS), the Arabs had

again begun to pollute the teachings of their forefather with the worship of idols. Encouraged by a man called Amr bin Luhay, they filled the Kabah and its surroundings with various idols.

Amr bin Abasa Sulami reported:

"I, in the state of the Ignorance (before embracing Islam) used to think that the people were in error and they were not on anything (which may be called the right path) and worshipped the idols. In the meanwhile I heard of a man in Makkah who was giving news (on the basis of his prophetic knowledge) so I sat on my ride and went to him. The Messenger of Allah (SAWS) was at that time hiding as his people had made life hard for him. I adopted a friendly attitude (towards the Makkans and thus managed) to enter Makkah and went to him (the Holy Prophet) and I said to him: 'Who are you?'

He said: 'I am a Prophet (of Allah).' I again said: 'Who is a Prophet?' He said: '(I am a Prophet in the sense that) I have been sent by Allah.' I said: 'What is that which you have been sent with?' He said: 'I have been sent to join ties of relationship (with kindness and affection), to break the idols, and to proclaim the oneness of Allah (in a manner that) nothing is to be associated with Him.'" [Bukhari: Book 04, Number 1812]

Source: https://daiyah.fandom.com/wiki/Destruction_of_Idols

Pre-Islamic Goddesses

In the Qur'an, Al-Lat is mentioned along with al-'Uzzá and Manāt in Sura 53:19–23.

The tribe of ʿād of Iram of the Pillars is also mentioned in Sura 89:5– 8, and archaeological evidence from Iram shows copious inscriptions devoted to her for the protection of a tribe by that name.

Al-lāt is also explicitly attested from early Islamic records discussing the pre-Islamic period. According to the Book of Idols (Kitāb al-ʾAṣnām) by Hishām ibn al-Kalbi, the pre-Islamic Arabs believed Al-lāt resided in the Kaʿbah and also had an idol inside the sanctuary.

Al-'Uzzá was also worshipped by the Nabataeans, who equated her with the Greek goddess Aphrodite Ourania (Roman Venus Caelestis). A stone cube at aṭ-Ṭā'if (near Mecca) was held sacred as part of her cult. She is mentioned in the Qur'an Sura 53:19 as being one of the goddesses that people worshiped.

The temple dedicated to al-'Uzzá and the statue itself was destroyed by Khalid ibn al Walid in Nakhla in 630 AD.

Shortly after the Conquest of Mecca, Muhammad began aiming at eliminating the last idols reminiscent of pre-Islamic practices.

He sent Khalid ibn Al-Walid during Ramadan 630 AD (8 AH) to a place called Nakhlah, where the goddess al-'Uzzá was worshipped by the tribes of Quraish and Kinanah. The shrine's custodians were from Banu

Shaiban. Al-'Uzzá was considered the most important goddess in the region.

Khalid set out with 30 horsemen to destroy the shrine. It appears that there were two idols of al-'Uzzá, one real and one fake. Khalid first located the fake and destroyed it, then returned to the Prophet to report that he had fulfilled his mission. ***"Did you see anything unusual?"*** asked the Prophet.

No," replied Khalid.

"Then you have not destroyed al-'Uzzá," said the Prophet. "Go again."

Angry at the mistake that he had made, Khalid once again rode to Nakhlah, and this time he found the real temple of al-'Uzzá.

The custodian of the temple of al-'Uzzá had fled for his life, but before forsaking his goddess he had hung a sword around her neck in the hope that she might be able to defend herself.

As Khalid entered the temple, he was faced by an unusual naked dark woman who stood in his way and wailed. Khalid did not stop to decide whether this woman might be there to seduce him or to protect the idol, so he drew his sword in the name of Allah and with one powerful stroke the woman was cut in two. He then smashed the idol, and returning to Mecca, gave the Prophet an account of what he had seen and done.

Then the Prophet said, ***"Yes, that was al-'Uzzá; and never again shall she be worshipped in your land."***

The pre-Islamic Arabs believed Manāt to be the goddess of fate. She was known by the cognate name Manawat to the Nabataeans of Petra, who equated her with the Graeco-Roman goddess Nemesis, and she was considered the wife of Hubal.

"The most ancient of all these idols was Manāt. The Arabs used to name their children 'Abd-Manāt and Zayd-Manāt. Manāt was erected on the seashore in the vicinity of al-Mushallal in Qudayd, between Medina and Mecca. All the Arabs used to venerate her and sacrifice before her. The Aws and the Khazraj, as well as the inhabitants of Medina and Mecca and their vicinities, used to venerate Manāt, sacrifice before her, and bring unto her their offerings... The Aws and the Khazraj, as well as those Arabs among the people of Yathrib and other places who took to their way of life, were wont to go on pilgrimage and observe the vigil at all the appointed places, but did not shave their heads. At the end of the pilgrimage, however, when they were about to return home, they would set out to the place where Manāt stood, shave their

heads, and stay there a while. They did not consider their pilgrimage completed until they visited Manāt." — Book of Idols, pp 12–14.

The temple of Manat was raided and the idol was destroyed on the orders of Muhammad, in the Raid of Sa'd ibn Zaid al-Ashhali, in January 630 AD (8AH, 9th month, of the Islamic Calendar), in the vicinity of al-Mushallal.

Some scholars have enumerated that Somnath Temple in India was attacked later by Muhammad Ghazni for an idol of Manat that had been secretly transferred to the said temple.

These three Pre-Islamic Goddesses look similar to Vedic Goddesses Lakshmi, Parvati, Saraswati.

A triple deity (sometimes referred to as threefold, tripled, triplicate, tripartite, triune or triadic, or as a trinity) is a deity associated with the number three.

Such deities are common throughout world history; the number three has a long historical associations. The Triple Goddess has been adopted by many neopagans as one of their primary deities.

In common Neopagan usage the three female figures are frequently described as the Maiden, the Mother, and the Crone, each of which symbolizes both a separate stage in the female life cycle and a phase of the Moon, and often rules one of the realms of earth, underworld, and the heavens. These may or may not be perceived as aspects of a greater single divinity. The Goddess of Wicca's duo theistic theology is generally portrayed as the Triple Goddess of the Moon, her masculine consort being the Horned God.

Source: www.Booksfacts.com

It is a practice from the advent of Islam that the idols/ deities are to be destroyed. In fact in Mecca all the idols approximating to 360 relating to Moon god worshipped by the Kurshyas were destroyed before the building of mosque.

This illustrated manuscript depict the Muslim army after their conquest of Mecca, it also shows the destruction of the idols inside the Ka'aba. Muhammad himself is not depicted, as depicting a prophet is considered taboo in Islamic tradition.

Made in Kashmir, India, in 1808 CE. The manuscript

is part of the collection of the National Library of France (Bibliothèque nationale de France).

Source:

https://www.worldhistory.org/image/11528/muhammad-conquers-mecca--destroys-its-idols/

❑

CHAPTER 5

Legal Position Krishna Janmabhoomi and Shahi Idgah Mosque

To understand the legal position of Krishna Janmabhoomi at Mathura it becomes important to understand the legal status of Temples and Mosques in line with their own relevant religious tenets.

Status of Temples and Mosques

As per Sanatana Dharma, Temples are an integral part of the Hinduism without which Hinduism can't be imagined whereas Mosques are not considered integral part of Islam.

Temples are not mere prayer halls like mosques in Islam. Temples had a wide ambit area incorporating many rituals and ceremonies to be performed of the deity (archa vigrah) like adhivas, abhishek, bhoga offering, 8 times aratik performance etc.

The construction of the temple is based on the science of Vaastu Shastra unlike mosques which are built with no science. Vaastu Shastra is very scientific as is well accepted even by modern Engineers and Architects. As per Vaastu Shastra the deity of Ananta Shesha (snake expansion of Lord Vishnu made of copper is placed) in construction of Vishnu temple and other copper kalash in other temple construction etc. where the deity in the temple is established that place is known as garbh griha. Scientifically it is seen that wherever the temple is built that place has vibrant magnetic fields.

As per Vedic scripture, particularly in the Puranas, the result of giving donation or helping in temple construction are enumerated but in Quran its nowhere mentioned that what resultant fruit one will achieve by constructing the Mosque.

Events post Mughal rule in relation to Krishna Janmabhoomi

The demolition of Krishna Janmabhoomi temple i.e., birth place of Lord Krishna at Katra Keshav temple which was existing in 17th Century i.e., between

1658-1707 as recorded by Italian traveller Niccola Manucci who worked in Mughal Court, described demolition of temple by Aurangzeb in his Book ***"Storia do Mogor"*** or Mugal India 1653-1708 volume III page 244-245, Manucci records the fact that several important temples including Sri Krishna Janmabhoomi at Mathura were demolished by Aurangzeb.

After the death of Aurangzeb, Mathura came under the rule of Jats of Bharatpur. It was in 1803 Mathura came under British rule.

In 1815, the entire land of Katra Keshav Dev measuring 13.37 acres land was put for auction sale. Raja Patni Mal of Banaras was highest bidder. His bid was accepted. He purchased 13.37 acres land of Katra Keshav Dev in auction sale and became its owner. The name of Raja Patni Mal, was recorded in revenue and municipal record as owner in possession of property at Katra Keshav Dev measuring 13.37 acres land. The name of legal heirs/ descendants of Raja Patni Mal was recorded in Government record.

Then there were number of cases filed by Muslims questioning the auction sale, ownership and possession of Raja Patni Mal but all of them were dismissed. In between 1888 and 1893 there was considerable litigation on the opening of Vrindaban Railway. The eastern side of Katra Keshav Dev was demolished and compensation was awarded to Rai Narsing Das a descendant of Raja Patni Mal.

Then the Rai Kishan Das the heir of Raja Patni Mal filed Civil Suit No. 517 of 1928. In this suit it was also decided that Plaintiff was owner in possession of the land in dispute and the material lying thereon. The suit was finally decided by This Hon'ble High Court in Second Appeal No. 691 of 1932 vide judgment dated 2nd December 1935 it has been held that Raja Patni Mal and his heirs were rightful owners of 13.37 acres land of Katra Keshav Dev and Muslims had no right over any part of said land.

From the judgment and decrees passed by Courts, it was held that Raja Patni Mal and his heirs were the valid owners of the entire 13.37 acres land of Katra Keshav Dev and Shahi Idgah masjid or any Muslim had no right or title over the aforesaid land.

On 8th February 1944, Rai Kishan Das and Rai Anand Krishna, the heirs of Raja Patni Mal, executed a sale deed on consideration of ₹ 13,400/- paid by Jugal Kishore Birla transferred ownership and possession of 13.37 acres land of Katra Keshav Dev in favour of Mahamana Madan Mohan Malviya, Goswami Ganesh Dutt and Bhikhen Lalji Aattrey.

In pursuance of sale deed the aforesaid vendees came into possession over the entire land of Katra Keshav Dev.

Copy of Sale Deed Evidencing Same

मैं राय कृष्णदास, पिता का नाम स्वर्गवासी राय प्रह्लाददासजी और मेरा पुत्र राय आनंदकृष्ण, जाति वैश्य अग्रवाल, निवासी रामघाट, काशी के हैं. आगे हम लोगों की एक किता जमीन जिसका नंबर पहले बंदोबस्त सन् १३१२ फसली में २८१ था और हाल बंदोबस्त में २५५ है तथा जिसका रकबा १३ एकड़ ३७ डिसमल है और जो कटरा केशवदेव के नाम से विख्यात है, मथुरा में स्थित है. उक्त भूभाग को हमारे पूर्वज राजा पटनीमल्ल बहादुर ने कंपनी सरकार से १६ मार्च सन् १८१५ ई० को खरीद किया था और खरीददारी की तारीख से उसपर अपना पूर्ण स्वत्व तथा अधिकार रखते थे. उक्त राजा साहब के दो पुत्र राय श्रीकृष्ण तथा राय रामकृष्ण थे और उक्त राय श्रीकृष्ण के दो पुत्र राय नारायणदास तथा राय नरसिंहदास थे और उक्त राय रामकृष्ण के चार पुत्र राय केशवदास, राय सीताराम, राय पुरुषोत्तमदास और राय विष्णुचंद थे. उक्त राय श्रीकृष्ण और राय रामकृष्ण के देहावसान के पश्चात् उक्त भूभाग के अधिकारी तथा पूर्ण मालिक उन लोगों के उक्त छ पुत्र हुए और इन दोनों शाखाओं के बँटवारे में उक्त भूभाग के मालिक राय नारायणदास तथा राय नरसिंहदास हुए और उन्हीं का नाम भी सेवट इत्यादि पर चढ़ा था और उन्हीं का पूर्ण अधिकार उक्त भूभाग पर था तथा वही उसकी आय इत्यादि लेते रहे और उसका पूर्ण प्रबंध मालिकाना करते रहे, तत्पश्चात् उक्त दोनों भाइयों के बँटवारे में उक्त भूभाग राय नरसिंहदास के अंश में आया और उनके स्वत्व तथा अधिकार में रहा और उनके पश्चात् उनके एकमात्र पुत्र, मुझ राय कृष्णदास के पिता, राय प्रह्लाददास उक्त भूभाग के मालिक तथा अधिकारी हुए और अब हम दोनों, राय कृष्णदास और मेरे पुत्र राय आनंदकृष्ण उसके पूर्ण मालिक तथा एकमात्र स्वत्वाधिकारी हैं. सन् १९२० ई० में जब कटरा केशवदेव के एक हिस्से पर स्थित गंगामंदिर की मरम्मत उसके मालिक पंडित प्रह्लाद जी, करा रहे थे तो मथुरा के मुसलमानों ने उन्हें रोका था और यह दावा किया था कि मंदिर की जमीन मुसलमानों की जायदाद है और वे उसपर काबिज हैं. यह मामला अदालत में पेश हुआ और अदालत ने फैसला दिया कि जमीन राजा पटनीमल्ल और उनके वारिसों की है, मुसलमानों

की नहीं. यह फैसला अपील में भी कायम रहा. देखो मुकदमा दीवानी नं० ७६, सन् १६२० ई०, अदालत सब जजी, मथुरा. सन् १६२८ ई० में मथुरा के मुसलमानों ने कटरा केशवदेव की जमीन पर फिर अपना हक कायम करने की कोशिश की थी लेकिन वे नाकामयाब रहे. मुंसिफी से हाईकोर्ट तक हार गए और तीनों अदालतों ने यह फैसला दिया कि यह जमीन राजा पटनीमल्ल के वंशज हमलोगों की है. देखो मुकदमा दीवानी नं० ५४७, १६२८ ई०, अदालत मुंसिफी, मथुरा, मुकदमा अपील नं० १३१, १६३२ ई०, अदालत सब जजी, मथुरा और मुकदमा अपील नं० ६६१, १६३५ ई०, अदालत हाईकोर्ट, इलाहाबाद. उक्त भूभाग की बिक्री आदि करने का हम लोगों को पूरा अधिकार है. उक्त भूभाग से हम लोगों को कोई विशेष आय नहीं है और बनारस से दूर होने के कारण उसके प्रबंध तथा देखभाल में बहुत असुविधा पड़ती है और व्यय अधिक होता है तथा इस समय उसको लेने के लिये महामना श्री पं० मदनमोहन मालवीय जी, सभापति, अखिल भारतीय सनातनधर्म महासभा, काशी, गोस्वामी गणेशदत्त जी, प्रधान मंत्री, सनातनधर्म प्रतिनिधि सभा, पंजाब, लाहौर और डा० भीखनलालजी आत्रेय, प्रोफेसर, फिलासफी, हिंदू विश्वविद्यालय, काशी उद्यत हैं तथा वे उसको लेकर श्रीकृष्ण जन्मभूमि मंदिर का, जो आदि में इस भूभाग पर था तथा जिसको औरंगजेब ने गिरवा दिया था, यथासंभव उद्धार करना चाहते हैं जो कि हमको भी अभीष्ट है क्योंकि इसी उद्देश्य से हमारे मूल पुरुष उक्त राजा साहब ने इसका क्रय किया था. उक्त भूभाग का मूल्य १३४००रु० अंकन तेरह हजार चार सौ रुपए में सर्व के उक्त महामना श्री पं० मदनमोहन मालवीय जी, गो० गणेशदत्तजी तथा डा० भीखनलाल जी आत्रेय दे रहे हैं जो कि हमलोगों की समझ में सब स्थिति को देखते हुए, उचित है. इसलिये हम दोनों अर्थात् राय कृष्णदास और राय आनंद कृष्ण प्रसन्नतापूर्वक बिना किसी दबाव के भली भांति समझ बूझकर यह विक्रयपत्र उक्त भूभाग के विषय में, जिसका विवरण ऊपर लिखा हुआ है और जिसकी चौहद्दी नीचे दी हुई है, उक्त महामना श्री पं० मदनमोहन मालवीय जी महाराज, गो० गणेशदत्त जी तथा डा० भीखनलाल जी आत्रेय के प्रति लिखकर अपने को तथा अपने प्रतिनिधियों एवं उत्तराधिकारियों को नीचे लिखी शर्तों से बद्ध करते हैं,

१. यह कि, संपूर्ण मूल्य रु० १३४००, अंकन तेरह हजार चार सौ रुपए जो ते हुआ है उसमें से

तीन रुपया आठ आना

अंकन तेरह हजार रुपए जरिए क्रास चेक नं० डी.टी.००५२२६ तारीख १८ जनवरी १९४४ ई०, ऊपर, दि यूनाइटेड कमर्शल बैंक लि०, दिल्ली, सब रजिस्ट्रार मथुरा के सामने, रजिस्ट्री के समय, हम लोगों को अपने मुख्तारआम श्री विश्वनाथ सिंह के हस्ते मिले हैं. अब कुछ बाकी नहीं है.

२. यह कि, आज की मिति से उक्त भूभाग पर उक्त महामना श्री पं० मदनमोहन मालवीय जी, गो० गणेशदत्त जी, तथा ला० भीखनलाल जी आत्रेय का पूर्ण स्वत्व और अधिकार हमलोगों ने करा दिया. उनको अधिकार है कि अपने नाम आवश्यक कागदों पर चढ़वा लेवें और मंदिर के जीर्णोद्धार के उद्देश्य को ध्यान में रखते हुए जिस प्रकार चाहें कटरा केशवदेव का उपयोग करें. अब उसमें हम लोगों का कोई अधिकार बाकी नहीं रहा और न उससे हम लोगों का कोई संबंध रहा. जो जो अधिकार उक्त भूभाग में हम लोगों को प्राप्त थे वे अब इस बैनामे के व्दारा उक्त महामना पं० मदनमोहन मालवीय जी, गो० गणेशदत्त जी तथा ला० भीखनलाल जी आत्रेय को प्राप्त हो गए हैं.

३. यह कि, उक्त भूभाग हर प्रकार के बार देन से रहित है. यदि कोई बात इसके विरुद्ध प्रकट हो जिसके कारण कोई बार उक्त महामना श्री पं० मदनमोहन मालवीय जी, गो० गणेशदत्त जी तथा ला० भीखनलाल जी आत्रेय या उनके प्रतिनिधियों या उत्तराधिकारियों को देना पड़े तो उसे व्यय और नुकसानी सहित देने के लिये हम दोनों विक्रेता व हमारे प्रतिनिधि तथा उत्तराधिकारी बाध्य होंगे. परंतु इसके अतिरिक्त और किसी बात की जिम्मेदारी हम लोगों तथा हमारे प्रतिनिधियों तथा उत्तराधिकारियों पर नहीं रहेगी. जो और जितने अधिकार इस समय कटरा केशवदेव में हमलोगों को प्राप्त हैं उन सबको इस विक्रयपत्र व्दारा उक्त तीनों सज्जनों को देते हैं.

इसलिये यह विक्रयपत्र हमलोगों ने लिख दिया कि प्रमाण रहे और समय पर काम आवे.

चौहद्दी उक्त कटरा केशवदेव की, जिसका बैनामा किया जाता है, पूरब, रेलवे लाइन, बी.बी.सी.आई. रेलवे. पच्छिम, मंदिर जो कि केशवदेव के नाम से प्रसिद्ध है., उत्तर, जमीन नजूल. दक्षिण, जमीन उफ्तादा व कच्चा रास्ता, दगरा.

टाइपकर्ता [illegible], [illegible] सभा, काशी, २/१/१९४४

Reg. fee 22/8/- S.C. 5/10/- 2/4/- /8/ 30/12/

for Mukhtaram of Rai Krishna Das and Anand Krishna. St.

Thakur Vishwanath Singh s/o Thakur Dwarka Singh [illegible] Zamindari and service resident of Mauza Gurera [illegible]

pargana [illegible]

General Power of Attorney [illegible] at the office the Sub-Registrar of Banaras as No. 10 of 1944 at the office of Sub-Registrar, Muttra this the 17th day of February 1944 between the hours of 2 and 3. P.M.

[illegible] S.R. Muttra 17.2.44.

[illegible]

Execution admitted by the said Thakur Vishwanath Singh on behalf of Rai Krishna Das, profession Zamindari s/o Rai Prahlad Das of Banaras and Rai Anand Krishna profession Zamindari s/o Rai Krishna Das through the said power of Attorney, and receipt of consideration acknowledged, out of which a cheque for Rs 13000/- (thirteen thousand only) No. DT 005226 dated Delhi 10th January 1944 on the United Commercial Bank Ltd. was paid before me in favour of Rai Krishna Das. The said Thakur Vishwanath Singh has been identified by Madan Mohan Chaturvedi s/o Pt. Gadadhar Ram [illegible] Brij Mahavidyalay Trust, Brindaban who is personally known to me and by Indra Dev profession Service s/o B. Ram Chand, caste Vaish, r/o Subzi Mandi, Delhi.

Indra Dev

Then there was another suit which is Civil Suit No. 4 (Four) of 1946 was filed on behalf of Trust Shahi Idgah Masjid against Pt. Madan Mohan Malviya and other's questioning the sale deed dated 8.2.1944 on the ground of pre-emption (judicial principle of supremacy of Right to purchase in advance than others). This suit was dismissed on the basis of compromise and it was further directed that the judgment dated 2.12.1935 passed by Hon'ble High Court in Second Appeal No. 691 of 1932 would be binding on parties.

Late Sh. Jugal Kishore Birla had taken pledge to construct a glorious temple at Katra Keshav Dev glorifying the birth place of Lord Shree Krishna and for this purpose he had purchased the land of Katra Keshav Dev measuring 13.37 acres through sale deed dated 8.2.1944 in the name of revered Hindu leader Pt. Mahana Madan Mohan Malviya, Goswami Ganesh Duttji and Bhikhen Lalji Aattrey.

Shri Jugal Kishore Birla created a Trust in the name of 'Shree Krishna Janmabhoomi Trust' on 21.2.1951 through Trust deed which was registered on 9.3.1951 in the office of Sub-Registrar Mathura.

He dedicated the entire land of Katra Keshav Dev measuring 13.37 acres to the deity Lord Shree Krishna Virajman.

The settlement between the Shri Krishna Janmabhoomi Trust and Shahi Idgah Masjid underwent and approx. 2 acre land is given to Shahi Idgah Masjid which is trampling of the Hindus' right to worship.

Copy of Settlement Deed

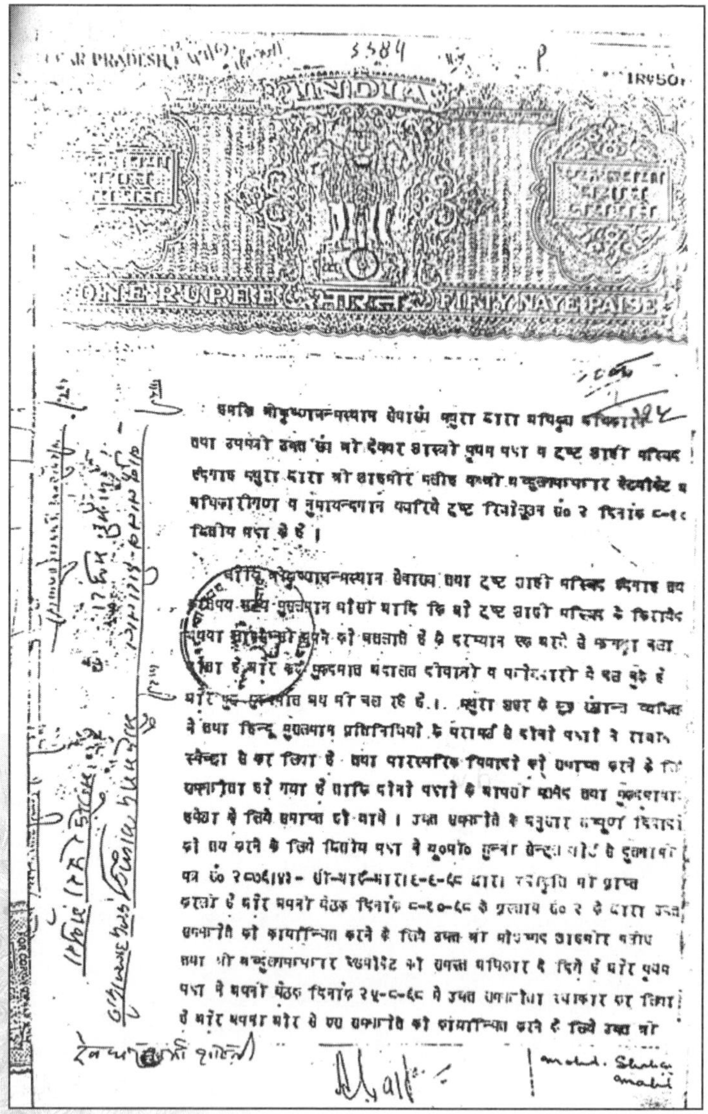

UTTAR PRADESH 5584 IRs50

INDIA

ONE RUPEE भारत FIFTY NAYE PAISE

चूँकि श्रीकृष्ण जन्मस्थान सेवा संघ मथुरा द्वारा अधिकृत अधिकारी तथा उसकी उक्त संघ की ओर से देकर इसको प्रथम पक्ष व ट्रस्ट शाही मस्जिद ईदगाह मथुरा द्वारा श्री शाहमीर मलीह तथा श्री अब्दुल गफ्फार एडवोकेट व अधिकारीगण व नुमायन्दगान बजरिये ट्रस्ट रिज़ोल्यूशन सं० २ दिनांक ८-१० द्वितीय पक्ष कहे हैं।

चूँकि श्रीकृष्ण जन्मस्थान सेवा संघ तथा ट्रस्ट शाही मस्जिद ईदगाह तथ कतिपय अन्य मुसलमान भाई आदि कि जो ट्रस्ट शाही मस्जिद के फरीक [illegible] इनके दरम्यान एक अर्से से झगड़ा चला आ रहा है और कई मुकदमात अदालत दीवानी व फौजदारी में चल चुके हैं और कुछ मुकदमात अब भी चल रहे हैं। मथुरा शहर के कुछ शान्त व्यक्तियों ने तथा हिन्दू मुसलमान प्रतिनिधियों के परामर्श से दोनों पक्षों ने राजी स्वेच्छा से कर लिया है तथा पारस्परिक विवादों को समाप्त करने के लिए समझौता कर गया है ताकि दोनों पक्षों के आपसी विवाद तथा मुकदमात हमेशा के लिये समाप्त हो जावें। उक्त समझौते के अनुसार सम्पूर्ण विवादों को तय करने के लिये द्वितीय पक्ष ने यू०पी० सुन्नी सेन्ट्रल बोर्ड के पत्र सं० २८०६/१४३- सी-आर-बी/ता०१६-६-६८ द्वारा स्वीकृति भी प्राप्त करली है और अपनी बैठक दिनांक ८-१०-६८ के प्रस्ताव सं० २ के द्वारा उक्त समझौते को कार्यान्वित करने के लिये उक्त श्री मो० शाहमीर मलीह तथा श्री अब्दुल गफ्फार एडवोकेट को समस्त अधिकार दे दिये हैं और प्रथम पक्ष ने अपनी बैठक दिनांक २५-८-६८ में उक्त समझौता स्वीकार कर लिया है और अपनी ओर से इस समझौते को कार्यान्वित करने के लिये उक्त श्री

२

१४५

देकर शाखो को सम्पूर्ण अधिकार दे दिये है । उक्त समझौते के कार्यान्वित करने में कुछ समय लगेगा अत: यह उचित तथा आवश्यक समझा गया है कि जो समझौता होगया है उसकी बाबत एक इकरारनामा बाकायदा तहरीर करके रजिस्टरी करा लिया जावे । अत: हम दोनो पक्ष स्वेच्छा से सब सोच समझ कर तथा दोनो संस्थाओ की स्वीकृति से यह इकरारनामा निम्न शर्तों सहित तहरीर किये देते है कि जिसकी पाबन्दी हम दोनो पक्षो पर समान रूप से होगी तथा दोनो पक्षो का कर्तव्य होगा कि उसको पूर्णरूप से कार्यान्वित करदे ।

१- यह कि ईदगाह की कच्ची कुरसी की उत्तर व दक्खिन की दीवारो को पूर्व की ओर रेलवे लाइन तक बढा लिया जावे । इन दोनो दीवारो का निर्माण ट्रस्ट शाही मस्जिद ईदगाह करेगा ।

२- यह कि दीवारो के बाहर उत्तर व दक्खिन की ओर जो घोसी आदि की मुस्लिम आबादी है उसको ट्रस्ट शाही मस्जिद ईदगाह अपनी जिम्मेदारी पर खाली करा कर श्रीकृष्णजन्मस्थान सेवासंघ को सौप देगा और इनकी मिल्कियत से ट्रस्ट शाही मस्जिद ईदगाह आदि उनके दावेदार घोसी वगैरह या अन्य किसी मुसलमान का कोई वास्ता नही रहेगा और यह प्रथम पक्ष की मिल्कियत समझी जावेगी । और इसी तरह उत्तर दक्खिन की दीवारो के भीतर की भूमि की मिल्कियत से श्रीकृष्ण जन्मस्थान सेवासंघ का कोई वास्ता नहीं रहेगा ।

३

१२४

३- यह कि ईदगाह की कच्ची कुरसी के पश्चिमी-उत्तरी कोने में जो भूमि श्रीकृष्णजन्मस्थान सेवासंघ की है और जो नक्शे में ए०बी०सी०डी० द्वारा दिखाया गया है उसमें ट्रस्ट शाही मस्जिद ईदगाह अपनी कच्ची कुरसी को चौकोर कर लेगा और वह उसी की मिल्कियत मानी जायेगी।

४- यह कि दक्षिण की ओर जो भीति का मलवा जिस पर मुकदमाबाजी हो रही है उस मलवे को दिनांक १५ अक्टूबर १९६८ तक ट्रस्ट शाही मस्जिद ईदगाह उठा लेगा और उस भूमि पर श्रीकृष्णजन्मस्थान सेवासंघ का कब्जा हो जायेगा।

५- यह कि जो मकानात उत्तर दक्षिण वाली दीवारों के बाहर घोसियों आदि की मुस्लिम आबादी के हैं तथा जिन मकानों का बैनामा घोसियों से ट्रस्ट मस्जिद ईदगाह ने अपने हक में करा लिया है उनको ट्रस्ट शाही मस्जिद ईदगाह १५ अक्टूबर १९६८ तक खाली करा कर श्रीकृष्णजन्मस्थान सेवासंघ को सौंप देगा। यह कार्य पूरा होने पर ही ईदगाह ट्रस्ट दीवारें आदि बना सकेगा। इन दीवारों में तथा कच्ची कुरसी की दीवारों में श्रीकृष्णजन्मस्थान सेवासंघ की ओर कोई दरवाजा या जंगला खिड़की आदि ट्रस्ट शाही मस्जिद ईदगाह नहीं लगा सकेगा और न इनमें कोई मोरी या परनाला ही श्रीकृष्ण जन्मस्थान सेवासंघ की ओर निकाल सकेगा। इसी प्रकार श्रीकृष्णजन्मस्थान सेवासंघ भी ऐसा कोई कार्य नहीं करेगा।

६- यह कि ईदगाह के जो परनाले श्रीकृष्णजन्मस्थान सेवासंघ की ओर पश्चिम की तरफ पड़ते हैं उनको श्रीकृष्णजन्मस्थान सेवासंघ अपने खर्चे से पाइप लगा कर उनका पानी ईदगाह की कच्ची कुरसी पर मोड़ देगा और उसके बाद उस पानी को अपने खर्च से पक्की नाली बनवा कर पूर्व की ओर मस्जिद के पूर्वी दरवाजे तक, कच्ची कुर्सी की हद तक, पहुंचा देगा। मस्जिद ईदगाह की दीवारों में पाइप लगाने में ट्रस्ट शाही मस्जिद ईदगाह को कोई एतराज नहीं होगा। इस काम को पूरा कराने में ट्रस्ट शाही मस्जिद ईदगाह का प्रतिनिधि साथ होगा और उसकी सलाह मानी जायेगी।

७- यह कि रेलवे की जो भूमि श्रीकृष्णजन्मस्थान सेवासंघ एक्वायर करा रहा है उसके एक्वायर होने पर ईदगाह के सामने जो भूमि उत्तर दक्षिण की दीवारों से

४

2.0.45
8
22

के भीतर आयेगी उसको भी श्रीकृष्णजन्मस्थान सेवासंघ ट्रस्ट शाही मस्जिद ईदगाह को देदेगा और वह निर्विवाद द्वितीय पक्ष समझी जावेगी।

८- यह कि जो भूमि कच्ची कुरसी के आगे पूर्व की ओर ई० एस० बी० एव आई० जे० के० एल० तथा पश्चिम उत्तर के कोने में एच०जी०एफ०ई० द्वारा प्रदर्शित की गयी है और जिसको श्रीकृष्णजन्मस्थान सेवासंघ ने ट्रस्ट शाही मस्जिद ईदगाह के हक में छोड़ा है उसे संलग्न नक्शे में तिरछी लाइनों द्वारा दिखाया गया है।

९- यह कि दोनों पक्षों की ओर से जो मुकदमे चल रहे हैं उनमें समझौते की शर्तें पूरी हो जाने पर दोनों पक्ष राजीनामा इसी समझौते के मुताबिक दाखिल कर देंगे।

१०- यह कि दोनों पक्षों को यह अधिकार होगा कि यदि कोई पक्ष इस इकरारनामा की शर्तों की पाबन्दी नहीं करता है तो वह अदालत द्वारा या जिस प्रकार भी संभव हो उनको कार्यान्वित करा ले। इसमें दूसरे पक्ष को कोई आपत्ति न होगी और वह कोई आपत्ति न कर सकेगा।

अतः यह इकरारनामा एक प्रतिलिपि सहित दोनों पक्षों ने अपनी रजामन्दी से लिख दिया कि प्रमाण रहे तथा समय पर काम आवे।

तहरीर तारीख १२ अक्टूबर १९६८ ई० टाइप किया द्वारिकाप्रसाद चतुर्वेदी द्वारा

प्रतिलिपि

देवधर शर्मा शास्त्री

Mohd. Shah-amir Maalik

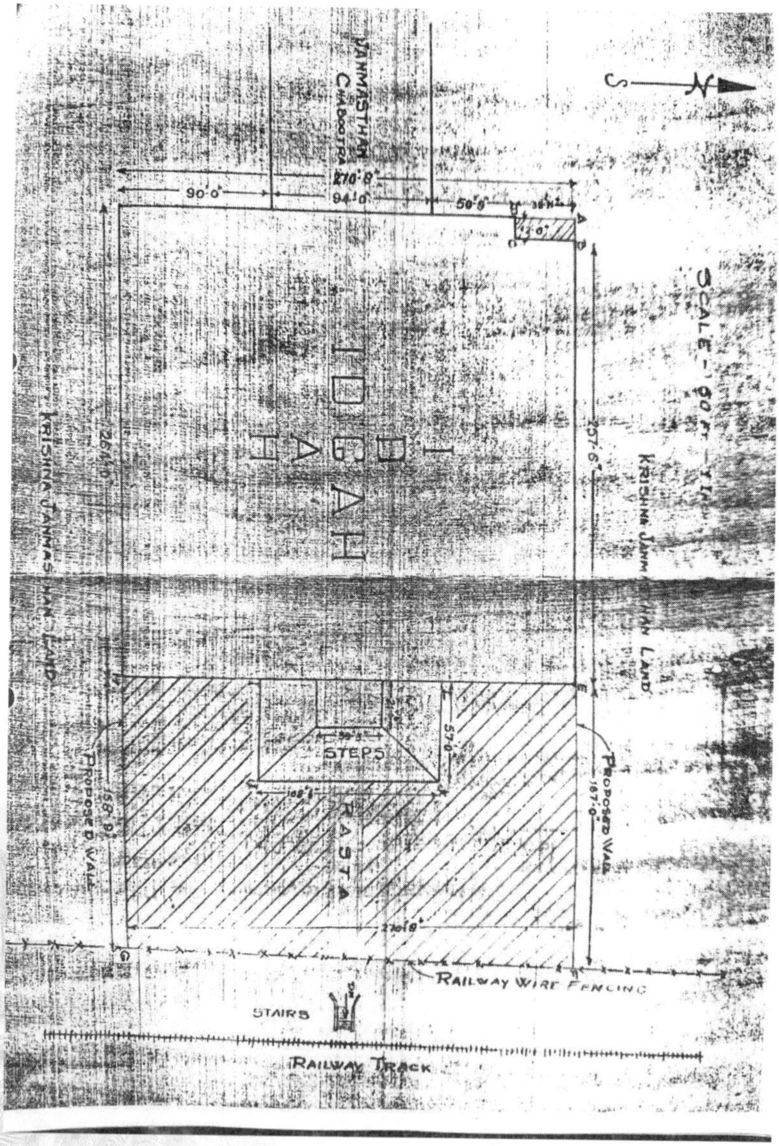
JANMASTHAN CHABOOTRA
IDGAH
KRISHNA JANMASTHAN LAND
KRISHNA JANMASTHAN LAND
STEPS
RASTA
PROPOSED WALL
PROPOSED WALL
RAILWAY WIRE FENCING
STAIRS
RAILWAY TRACK
270'-8"
90'-0"
94'-0"
257'-6"
167'-0"
57'-0"

Legal and Logical reasoning behind Krishna Janmabhoomi status restoration

- In the case of Ismail Farooqui vs Union of India case [reported in (1994) 6 SCC 376], this Hon'ble Court observed: ***"It has been contended that a mosque enjoys a particular position in Muslim law and once a mosque is established and prayers are offered in such a mosque, the same remains for all time to come a property of Allah...and any person professing Islamic faith can offer prayer in such a mosque, and even if the structure is demolished, the place remains the same where namaz can be offered" [para 80]. The Constitution Bench rebutted this contention stating: "The correct position may be summarized thus: Under Mohåmmedan law applicable in India, the title to a mosque can be lost by adverse possession. A mosque is not an essential part of the practice of the religion of Islam and namaz (prayer) can be offered anywhere, even in the open. Accordingly, its acquisition is, not prohibited by the provisions in the Constitution of India. "***[para 82].
- The position in Islamic law is eye clearer – In Saudi Arabia the authorities demolish mosque to lay roads and build apartment building. Even the mosque where Islam's Prophet' Mohammed used to pray

was demolished. If a waqf falls into disrepair and is no longer of any benefit, such as if a house collapses and it is not possible to rebuild it, or the people of the village move away from a mosque so people no longer pray in the mosque, or it has become too small for the congregation and it is not possible to expand it where it is, or if its walls have developed cracks and it is not possible to repair them or part of them except by selling part of it, then it is permissible to sell part of it in order to repair the rest of it. If it is not possible to benefit from any part of it, it is permissible to of it and use the money to build another mosque.

- In Mecca, the Masjid al-Haram, the holiest site in Islam and a place where all Muslims are supposed to be equal, is now overshadowed by the Jabal Omar complex, a development of skyscraper apartments, hotels and an enormous clock tower. To build it, the Saudi authorities destroyed the Ottoman era Ajyad Fortress and the hill it stood on. Other historic sites lost include the Prophet's birthplace — now a library — and the house of his first wife, Khadijah, which was replaced with a public toilet block.
- Until recently out of the seven ancient mosques built to commemorate the Battle of the Trench — a key moment in the development of Islam — only two remain. Few years ago, a mosque which belonged to the Prophet's grandson was dynamited. Pictures

of the demolition that were secretly taken and smuggled out of the kingdom showed the religious police celebrating as the building collapsed.

- This question of the status of a temple-even if in ruins or without worship – had come up before the British Courts in a case of a smuggled-out bronze Nataraja statue which was up for auction in London. The Government of India had decided to file a case in the London trial court in 1986 for recovery. The Nataraja statue had by then been traced to a temple in ruins in Pathur, in Thanjavur district. A farmer named Ramamoorthi had in 1976 accidently unearthed it while digging mud with a spade near his hut.

  When the news spread, touts; of an antique dealer by name Ahmed Hussein reached him and paid a small sum and smuggled it out to London, where in 1982 they sold it to Bumper Development Corporation Private Limited. In turn the said Corporation sent it to the British Museum for appraisal and possible purchase. By then the Government of India was onto it and asked the UK government to take action.

- Thus, even if a temple is in ruins as the ASI had found, the Thanjavur temple were destroyed, as Ram Temple was under Babri mosque. Shahi Idgah Mosque exists on the area of Krishna Janmasthan. Any Hindu can sue on behalf of Lord Krishna in court for recovery of possession. No such ruling exists for the simple reason that a mosque is just a facilitation centre for reading namaz, and has no essentiality for Islam religion. It can be demolished and/or shifted as any building can and are being so today in Arab countries and other Islamic countries.

- A masjid is not an essential part of Islamic Practice. It's just a facility to offer Namaz. Namaz can be offered anywhere irrespective of place. Many Muslims can be seen offering Namaz on Roads, Railway Tracks and even other Public Places although which is not in accordance with Article 25 of Constitution of India as it hampers the public order.
- The Sources of Islamic foundation is Quran and Hadith. Where Hadith states-

I. Land should not be usurped for the Construction of a mosque. (land of Janmabhoomi usurped for Shahi Idgah Masjid)

II. Azaan must be called at least twice a day (which is not from Shahi Idgah Mosque).

III. A mosque must have a vazoo or place for abulation.

IV. No ringing of bells is permissible within the precincts of or in the area surrounding the mosque. (Mathura is city of temples)

V. On one plot of land, two religious places are impermissible. (if land of Krishna Janmabhoomi is usurped for mosque how it is possible for that mosque to exist).

- The Krishna Janmabhoomi temple platform (Chabutara) was used as it is to erect Mosque.
- There is a description about the gifting of railing by Dara Sikoh the brother of Aurangzeb which after the killing of Dara Sikoh Aurangzeb ordered to take it out from temple. Later he ordered to demolish whole Krishna Janmabhoomi temple also known as Katra Keshav Dev mandir.
- Once there was digging of the courtyard of the Shahi Idgah Mosque in August some few years back in which the workers reported existence of carved pillars and antiquities below the mosque.
- That there was no proper ASI excavation of Mathura after the one done by Late Mr. M.C. Joshi many years ago.
- Even on the Governments official website of Mathura District it is stated that Shahi Idgah Mosque is built after demolition of Krishna Janmabhoomi by Aurangzeb.
- Thus, even if a temple is in ruins as the ASI had found, the Thanjavur temple were destroyed, as Ram Temple was under Babri Mosque. Shahi idgah Mosque exists on the area of Krishna Janmasthan any Hindu can sue on behalf of Lord Krishna in court for recovery of possession.

The Shahi Eidgah in 1949 which was constructed on the raised plinth of the original temple destroyed by Aurangzeb

Conclusively, whether archaeological, historical, theological or legal in whichever way you perceive or observe the disputed site of Krishna Janmabhoomi where Shahi Idgah Mosque exists, specially the central dome of the Masjid is the actual place of birth of Supreme personality of Godhead Lord Krishna and was a place where Lord Keshavdeva was Virajman or installed.

Legal Battle over Krishna Janmabhoomi is on its progress from my side as a petitioner in Hon'ble Allahabad High Court.

Several Petitions/Applications are also pending in Mathura District Court where Hon'ble Allahabad High Court directed Mathura District Court to decide all the Petitions/Applications within 4 month's time. First among all these petitions in District court of Mathura was by one of my fraternity member Adv. Mahendra Pratap Singh's petition.

Numerous Legal experts are of the opinion that Places of Worship Act 1991 is an impediment for this case but in my personal opinion that's not at all a real impediment in restoration of Krishna Janmabhoomi as places of Worship Act 1991 as unconstitutional.

Since Case is in Court, I cannot decipher every argument and legal points in this book which are to be presented in court for the temple but yes substantial legal understanding is covered in the book.

Hope we will sooner or later see Lord Keshavdeva to get virajman at the actual spot/birth place of Lord Krishna which is Central Dome of the Shahi Idgah Mosque.

yatra yogeshvarah krsno

yatra pärtho dhanur-dharah

tatra srir vijayo bhütir

dhruvä nitir matir mama

Wherever there is Krishna, the master of all mystics, and wherever there is Arjuna, the supreme archer, there will also certainly be opulence, victory, extraordinary power, and morality. That is my opinion.

(Bhagvad Gita 18.78)

यतः कृष्णस्ततो धर्मो यतो धर्मस्ततो जयः

Where there is Krishna there is dharma and where there is dharma there is victory.

❑

References

1. Srimad Bhagvatam by A.C. Bhaktivedanta Swami Srila Prabhupada
2. Mathura Mahatmya
3. Mathura Memoir – F.S. Growse
4. Aurangzeb firmans stored at Bikaner Museum
5. Ayodhya Ram Mandir Judgement by Hon'ble Supreme Court
6. Dr. Subramanian Swamy's Petition for Ayodhya Ram Mandir
7. Masir-I-alamgiri
8. Indian Constitutional Law by M.P. Jain
9. Booksfacts.com
10. Islamic Law
11. https://islamqa.info/en/answers/20894/obligation-to-destroy- idols
12. https://daiyah.fandom.com/wiki/Destruction_of_Idols
13. https://www.theguardian.com/world/2015/jul/02/isis-militants- destroy-palmyra-stone-lion-al-lat
14. https://www.mei.edu/publications/death-buddhas-bamiyan

15. https://www.wisdomlib.org/south-asia/book/buddhist-records-of-the-western-world-xuanzang/d/doc220218.html

16. www.krishna.com

17. https://en.wikipedia.org/wiki/Aurangzeb#/media/File:Battle_ele phant.jpg

18. https://www.facebook.com/trueindology.org/photos pcb.1453699338163914/ 1453699228163925/?type=3 andtheater

19. Many of the Firmans and Paintings depicted in the book are preserved at Bikaner Museum, Rajasthan.

❑